Christmas

with MARTHA STEWART LIVING

Christmas

with MARTHA STEWART LIVING

VOLUME 1

THE BEST OF MARTHA STEWART LIVING

Special thanks to the many stylists, art directors, photographers,
writers, and editors whose inspirational ideas make up this volume.
Thanks also to the entire staff of MARTHA STEWART LIVING OMNIMEDIA and to everyone at
Oxmoor House, Clarkson Potter, Satellite Graphics, and Quebecor Printing whose
invaluable work helped produce this book.

Manufactured in the United States of America.
Library of Congress Catalog Number: 97-66605
ISBN 0-8487-1627-2 (hardcover)
0-8487-1639-6 (paperback)

Editor: Bruce Shostak
Designer: Linda Kocur
Writer: Amy Conway
Managing Editor: Kyle T. Blood
Endpaper Design: Eve Ashcraft

CONTENTS

INTRODUCTION

Our Christmases at home in Nutley, New Jersey, were always busy. Baking and cooking and gift-making took precedence over everything else in our house from the tenth of December until the first of January. Mother and I started baking fruitcakes and cookies and making mincemeat early in the month, and we didn't stop cracking nuts, sifting flour, and preserving fruits until we were absolutely sure that every one of our family's friends and relatives had a wonderful homemade gift.

Not only did we cook and bake, we sewed and crafted and hand-painted any number of very special projects that we added to our repertoire of presents. I remember painting metal trays with images of pansies, roses, and lily bouquets. My siblings and I hand-bound books that we gave as albums and diaries. We sewed and embroidered decorative Christmas stockings, and I even made ceramic vases and plates and boxes, which I gave proudly to my friends.

The decorations that adorned our house on Elm Place were all homemade and really nothing like the beautiful creations you will find in this book, but they were personal, traditional interpretations of the holiday season; we loved making them, and everybody enjoyed looking at them.

We would have several gatherings of friends and family during the month of December. Mother would cook Polish dishes that everyone loved—there would be stuffed cabbage and pierogi dumplings and kielbasa sausage. She would also bake the family babka and fruit-and-nut-studded stollen, and all of us would insist on piles of rich, buttery cookies. Dad would make hot mulled cider and dark red-wine punch, full of spices, and the neighbors would contribute Christmas cakes and puddings.

This book extends those traditions and elaborates on the basics we all knew as children. The craft projects are practical and beautiful, and the decorations are extraordinary in their usage of traditional materials in very untraditional ways. I hope you will enjoy adding them to your own family's repertoire. Merry, merry Christmas.

Martha Stewart

CHRISTMAS PLANNER

The countdown to Christmas officially begins just after Thanksgiving Day—though of course you can be on the lookout for gifts, decorations, and ideas all year long. The schedule below will help you organize the holiday preparations in your house, whether they are new projects from this book or cherished family traditions. In the four weeks leading up to Christmas and the weeks that follow, there's so much to do. Careful planning is what enables you to accomplish it all—and enjoy it, too.

4 weeks ahead

Shop for gifts; start making handmade gifts

Plant amaryllis and paperwhites for holiday blooms; plant extras to give as gifts

Print out Christmas-card address list; make new additions and update list on computer

Purchase craft supplies for gift wrapping, gift tags, and ornaments

Send holiday cards and gifts to friends overseas

3 weeks ahead

Plan holiday entertaining and menus

Send invitations for New Year's Day open house

Make or purchase Christmas cards; begin writing them

Start baking cookies and making candies

Make felt stockings

Make paper and aluminum ornaments

Make wreaths and garlands

2 weeks ahead

Mail Christmas cards and gifts

Unpack ornaments, lights, and decorations; check lights

Bring tree home from tree farm or lot

Set up and decorate Christmas tree

Decorate house, inside and out, with wreaths, garlands, and lights

Buy poinsettias

Bake and decorate cookie ornaments

Make gift tags, and start wrapping gifts

Choose holiday table linens, china, and silverware

1 week ahead

Purchase or make last-minute gifts

Finish wrapping gifts

Order roast from butcher for Christmas dinner

Purchase ingredients for holiday dinner

Make holiday flower arrangements

New Year's Day

Host open house

Christmas Day

Enjoy the holiday with friends and family

week after New Year's

Remove, pack up, and store all ornaments, decorations, and lights

Arrange for recycling of Christmas tree, or use for mulch or for covering perennial beds

Write thank-you notes

week before New Year's

Save and organize ribbons and boxes

Buy champagne for New Year's Eve

Purchase ingredients and prepared foods for New Year's open house

MARTHA'S CHRISTMAS FEAST

During the holidays, the house you know so well becomes a magical, welcoming place; the weeks before Christmas are a time for creating a new, surprising world indoors. Every year, sweet aromas emanate from the kitchen, boxes of ornaments emerge from closet shelves, a tree sprouts up in the living room, the dining room table becomes a wrapping station. While cheerful activity and a sense of anticipation fill the home, the backdrop to all the celebrations need not remain the same, year after year. Decorations, gift wrapping, and the holiday menu can all be reinvented, in part or in whole.

This Christmas, Martha Stewart's East Hampton home sparkles with silver and subtle pinks, instead of the classic red and green. The table is set with a mix of cherished china, crystal, and silver carefully collected over the years; as the stemware catches the candlelight, the table glows. Fresh pears, apples, and pomegranates with a coating of silver leaf mark each setting and fill glass bowls and cake stands around the room. The atmosphere is lavish and festive, and it is Christmas, even though there are almost as many fresh flowers as greenery in the house.

Appetites for the English-style feast Martha has planned for her guests are whetted by oysters on the half shell and flutes of champagne. Prime-rib roast, the main course, is accompanied by a golden-crusted Yorkshire pudding, a rich purée of brussels sprouts, and baked quinces stuffed with wild mushrooms. Wedges of robust Stilton and Lancashire cheeses are served with a sprinkling of pomegranate seeds. And a dessert buffet worthy of Dickens offers an enticing finish to the sumptuous meal—a feast that is truly a generous gift to anyone's guests. The gift requires time and effort, but, as Martha says, "You do it for the sake of Christmas."

ABOVE: Wide, supple ribbon cascades from a wreath hung behind an elegant 1930s French candelabra. PREVIOUS PAGES, LEFT AND RIGHT: The dining room is decorated in soft pinks and sparkling silvers rather than the expected holiday reds and greens; garlands framing the windows are smoky-blue *Acacia baileyana* leaves dotted with pink pepperberries. Small wrapped gifts are nestled beneath a Victorian smoke bell, originally used to snuff out candles.

ABOVE LEFT: Each place setting is marked by a silver-leafed piece of fruit, such as this pear, and a small spray of pepperberries; a crystal plate from the 1840s and a silver lustreware dinner plate are layered beneath them. Antique stemware adds more pale, shimmery beauty to the table. TOP: Martha presents a platter of English cheeses to her guests. ABOVE: A glass compote shows off jewel-like hard candies. FAR LEFT: Regal antique decanters are filled with Sauternes and claret wines. NEAR LEFT: Glass cake stands, stacked one upon another, form the base for a dramatic tower of more silvered fruit and pepperberries.

OYSTERS
with festive MIGNONETTE

serves 8

Look for oysters with tightly sealed shells; discard any that are open.

- *1 tablespoon pink peppercorns*
- *1 tablespoon green peppercorns*
- *1 tablespoon fennel seed, lightly toasted*
- *½ cup red-wine vinegar*
- *½ cup champagne vinegar*
- *½ teaspoon salt*
- *2 dozen fresh oysters*

1. In a small bowl, combine the peppercorns, fennel seed, vinegars, and salt.
2. Shuck oysters just before serving; arrange on bed of crushed ice. Drizzle oysters with mignonette, or serve on the side. Serve oysters immediately.

BRUSSELS SPROUT *purée*

serves 6 to 8

- *1 pound brussels sprouts (about 4 cups)*
- *½ cup heavy cream*
- *2 tablespoons unsalted butter*
- *1¼ teaspoons salt*
- *½ teaspoon freshly ground pepper*
- *¼ teaspoon freshly grated nutmeg*

1. Trim tough stems from brussels sprouts. With a knife, mark base of each brussels sprout with a shallow "x." Separate about twenty-five outer green leaves; set aside.
2. In pot of boiling salted water, cook sprouts until tender but still bright green, 6 to 8 minutes. Strain; transfer to a bowl of ice water.
3. Blanch reserved leaves in pot of boiling water, until bright green, 1 to 2 minutes. Strain; transfer to bowl of ice water. Drain; reserve. Transfer sprouts to food processor.
4. Heat cream and butter in saucepan over low heat until butter has melted. Add salt, pepper, and nutmeg; add to sprouts. Process until combined. Transfer to serving bowl; arrange reserved leaves around edge.

ABOVE: Freshly shucked oysters on a bed of ice glisten in their salty liquor; they are served with a festive mignonette, a vinegar sauce flecked with peppercorns and fennel seed. Glasses of champagne accompany this elegant but remarkably simple hors d'oeuvre. RIGHT: A traditional winter vegetable is transformed for the holidays: Brussels sprouts are puréed with heavy cream and butter and seasoned with salt, pepper, and nutmeg; some whole outer leaves were reserved to be scattered around the rich purée on the serving dish.

TOP: Fresh quinces, once a symbol of affection, are baked slowly in Madeira wine, then filled with a savory mixture of dried porcini and wild mushrooms spiked with more Madeira; thyme sprigs garnish the dish. ABOVE, LEFT TO RIGHT: Young Caius Pawson is "the best conversationalist at the table," according to Martha. Stephen Whitehead, a stylist, and Judy Morris, a friend and colleague of Martha's, enjoy the meal. Martha offers guest Catherine Pawson prime-rib roast.

baked QUINCES *with wild* MUSHROOMS *in a madeira* GLAZE

serves 8

1   lemon, cut in half

4   quinces

1½ cups Madeira

1½ teaspoons salt

½   teaspoon freshly ground pepper

1   ounce dried porcini mushrooms

3   tablespoons unsalted butter

1   medium onion, finely chopped

2   teaspoons minced fresh thyme leaves,
*   plus sprigs for garnish*

½   pound wild mushrooms, such as
*   shiitake or oyster, trimmed and cut*
*   into 1-inch pieces*

1. Heat oven to 350°. Juice lemon, and place juice and both halves in large bowl of water. One at a time, peel quinces, halve, and core; transfer each half to acidulated water. Arrange quince halves, cut-side up, in 8-by-13-inch roasting pan. Drizzle with 1 cup Madeira; season with ¾ teaspoon salt and ¼ teaspoon pepper. Pour 2 cups water into pan. Cover tightly with foil. Bake until tender and translucent, about 1½ hours.

2. Meanwhile, place porcini mushrooms in bowl, cover with 1 cup boiling water; let stand until soft, about 30 minutes. Remove from water, reserving liquid; chop finely.

3. Heat the butter in large sauté pan over medium heat. Add onion; cook, stirring, until translucent, about 5 minutes. Add porcini mushrooms, minced thyme, and wild mushrooms; cook over medium heat, stirring until mushrooms release liquid, about 10 minutes. Reduce heat to medium low; add reserved porcini liquid, remaining ½ cup Madeira, ¼ teaspoon salt, and ¼ teaspoon pepper. Continue to cook over low heat until liquid is reduced to glaze and mushrooms are tender, 8 to 10 minutes. Transfer to large bowl.

4. Heat oven to 325°. Cover each quince with mushroom mixture, so mixture almost spills over. Cover with foil; heat in oven 30 minutes longer. Remove foil; bake 10 to 15 minutes. Serve garnished with thyme sprigs.

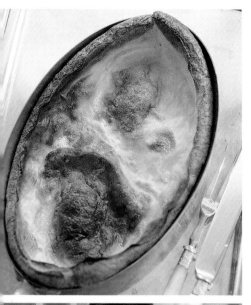

TOP: Yorkshire pudding, the classic English complement to roast beef, is like an overgrown popover, made from a simple batter of eggs, flour, salt, and meat drippings, which puffs up beautifully and develops a delicate golden crust in the oven. ABOVE: Guest John Pawson, a London-based architect, serves the pudding. OPPOSITE: The mix of rich and hearty flavors at Martha's traditional English Christmas dinner includes prime rib, Yorkshire pudding, baked stuffed quinces, and puréed brussels sprouts.

prime-rib ROAST

serves 6 to 8

To ensure even cooking, roast must be left at room temperature (about two hours) before being placed in the oven. For more detailed instructions on roasting prime rib, see page 124.

1   three-rib prime-rib roast, first cut,
    trimmed and tied
2   tablespoons coarse salt
1   tablespoon freshly ground pepper
3   short ribs, tied
1½ cups dry red wine

1. Place oven rack on lower level. Heat oven to 450°. Rub roast all over with salt and pepper. Transfer to heavy 13-by-16-inch metal roasting pan. Arrange fat-side up. Place short ribs in pan. (A nonstick pan will yield fewer cooked-on bits for flavorful juices.)
2. Cook 20 minutes. Reduce oven to 325° and continue cooking until instant-read thermometer inserted in thick end of roast (not touching a bone) reaches 115°, about 1 hour and 25 minutes. If it hasn't, return to oven; check temperature at 10-minute intervals.
3. Transfer roast to platter; set aside in warm spot for juices to collect. (As roast rests, temperature will increase about 10°.) Do not tent, or crust will get soggy. Adjust oven to 425°.
4. Pour fat and all the drippings out of pan into a fat separator, and set aside. Reserve the pan drippings for Yorkshire Pudding (recipe follows).
5. Place roasting pan over medium-high heat. Pour wine into pan; scrape bottom with wooden spoon, scooping up crispy bits to deglaze pan. Cook until reduced by half, 5 to 8 minutes. Place a fine sieve in heatproof bowl. Pour juices into the strainer. Using wooden spoon, press down on the solids to extract juices. Discard solids. Cover bowl tightly; keep warm by placing in barely simmering saucepan with 1 inch water. Serve warm juices with roast.

yorkshire PUDDING

serves 8

Yorkshire-pudding batter needs to be cold. Make it a day ahead, and refrigerate. For more detailed instructions, see page 124.

2   cups all-purpose flour
1   teaspoon salt
6   large eggs
2½ cups milk

1. Sift together flour and salt. Place in bowl; make a well, and place eggs in center. Slowly whisk eggs into flour mixture until a paste forms. Gradually whisk in ½ cup milk. Gradually whisk in remaining 2 cups milk. Cover with plastic; chill in the refrigerator at least 4 hours, or overnight.
2. When roast is finished, set oven at 425°. When pan has been deglazed, pour ¼ cup reserved pan drippings into roasting pan. Heat pan and drippings until very hot, about 5 minutes. Remove batter from refrigerator, and whisk well; quickly pour into hot pan. Cook until crisp and golden, 20 to 30 minutes. Serve warm with Prime-Rib Roast.

ABOVE: These desserts are a feast for the eyes after an already dazzling meal. A gingerbread trifle is layered with caramelized pears and cognac custard (center rear). Miniature baba au rhum, yeast cake soaked in rum syrup, is also flavored with ginger (left); extra syrup is served on the side (right). Candied chestnuts, known as marrons glacés (front), are an indulgent treat; look for them in gourmet stores.

ginger BABA AU RHUM

makes about 20 mini baba

These miniature versions of baba au rhum are made in mini brioche molds.

- *1 cup all-purpose flour, plus extra if dough gets sticky*
  Pinch of salt
- *¼ cup milk*
- *1 cup plus 4 teaspoons granulated sugar*
- *¼ ounce instant yeast*
- *2 large eggs*
- *3 tablespoons unsalted butter, melted, plus extra to coat molds*
- *4 teaspoons large-crystal sugar*
- *6 tablespoons rum*
- *1 one-inch piece fresh ginger, peeled, cut into four pieces*

1. Sift flour and salt into large bowl. In smaller bowl, combine warmed milk (110°), 4 teaspoons granulated sugar, and yeast. Let sit 5 minutes until foamy; stir. With wooden spoon, combine yeast mixture into flour. Add 1 egg, lightly beaten, and butter. Stir 5 minutes; dough will still be sticky. Cover; set in warm place 45 minutes, until doubled.

2. Meanwhile, heat oven to 425°. Beat dough with wooden spoon to remove air bubbles, adding 1 to 2 tablespoons flour if needed. Turn out dough onto lightly floured board. Form into 1-inch balls with floured hands. Place dough in well-buttered 1-by-2-inch molds. Cover, and let proof for 10 minutes. Whisk remaining egg with 1 tablespoon water. Brush the baba au rhum with the egg glaze, and sprinkle with large-crystal sugar. Bake about 10 minutes, until golden.

3. Meanwhile, combine remaining 1 cup granulated sugar, ¼ cup water, rum, and ginger in small saucepan. Stir over medium heat until sugar dissolves, about 3 minutes. Cook 5 minutes more. Set aside to steep. When baba are golden brown, remove from oven. Strain syrup into a large bowl. Turn baba out of pan and into syrup to soak. May be made up to this point 3 to 4 hours ahead. Serve baba in syrup at room temperature.

gingerbread TRIFLE *with*
cognac CUSTARD *and* PEARS

serves 8

2⅓ *cups sifted all-purpose flour*

1½ *teaspoons baking soda*

¼ *teaspoon salt*

1½ *teaspoons ground ginger*

1½ *teaspoons ground cinnamon*

8 *tablespoons (1 stick) unsalted butter,*
    cut into 8 pieces, plus 4 tablespoons

1½ *cups sugar*

2 *large eggs, at room temperature*

¾ *cup unsulfured molasses*

¾ *cup nonfat buttermilk*

1 *lemon*

10 *ripe pears, such as Bosc or Anjou*

1 *recipe Cognac Custard (recipe follows)*

1. Heat oven to 350°. Butter 9-inch-round-by-2-inch-tall cake pan; line with parchment.

2. Sift together flour, baking soda, salt, 1 teaspoon ginger, and 1 teaspoon cinnamon in a large bowl, and set aside.

3. Beat 8 tablespoons butter in electric mixer on medium-high speed until lightened, 3 to 4 minutes. Scrape down sides of bowl with rubber spatula. Add ½ cup sugar, ¼ cup at a time; scrape down sides after each addition. Beat until fluffy, 3 to 4 more minutes. Add eggs, one at a time, beating 1 minute after each addition. Slowly add molasses, beating on medium speed, about 10 seconds. Slowly pour in buttermilk; beat to combine.

4. On low speed, slowly add reserved flour mixture in three parts, beating to combine after each addition. Transfer to prepared pan. Bake 35 to 45 minutes, until cake tester inserted into center comes out clean. Let cool on wire rack. Gingerbread may be made 2 days ahead or kept frozen for 1 month.

5. Juice lemon; place juice and both halves in large bowl of cold water. One at a time, peel pears, quarter, core, and cut into 1-to-1½-inch chunks; transfer to acidulated water.

6. Drain pears; transfer half to 12-inch skillet. Add ½ cup sugar, 2 tablespoons butter, ¼ teaspoon ginger, and ¼ teaspoon cinnamon. Place over high heat; sauté, stirring, until

sugar and butter melt and form caramel, 4 to 5 minutes. Reduce heat to medium high, cover, and continue cooking 10 more minutes, stirring occasionally. Transfer pears and liquid to large bowl to cool; repeat with remaining pears, ½ cup sugar, 2 tablespoons butter, ¼ teaspoon ginger, and ¼ teaspoon cinnamon. Let cool completely.

7. Slice gingerbread into three rounds of equal thickness. Cut each round into eight triangles. Line bottom of trifle bowl with eight triangles of gingerbread; trim to fit if needed. Spoon 1 cup Cognac Custard over gingerbread, followed by 2 cups pears. Repeat process in two groups, layering with remaining gingerbread, custard, and pears.

cognac CUSTARD

makes 3⅓ cups

9 *large egg yolks*

¾ *cup sugar*

4½ *tablespoons all-purpose flour*

3 *cups milk*

¾ *teaspoon pure vanilla extract*

3 *tablespoons cognac*

1. Combine yolks and sugar in bowl of electric mixer. Beat on medium high until mixture is pale yellow and thick, 2 to 3 minutes. Reduce speed; add flour; beat to combine.

2. Meanwhile, bring milk to a boil in a medium saucepan. Slowly pour half the milk into egg mixture; beat until smooth. Pour mixture back into saucepan; set over medium heat. Whisk until mixture comes to a boil, 6 to 8 minutes. Transfer to large bowl. Stir in vanilla and cognac. Let cool. Cover with plastic wrap, and place in the refrigerator until needed or up to three days.

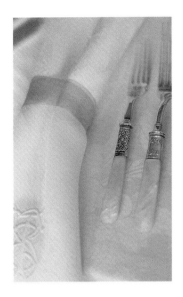

ABOVE: Lengths of pink ribbon tied around monogrammed napkins take the place of formal napkin rings; pearl-handled cutlery brings a pale shimmer to the rich mix of textures and subtle colors on the dining table.

TOP: Catherine Pawson finishes the meal with dessert and a glass of Sauternes. ABOVE: An unusual 1920s centerpiece encircles a nineteenth-century blown-glass bowl filled with silvered fruit and pink pepperberries.

apricot-lemon STEAMED PUDDING
with kumquat MARMALADE

serves 8

This recipe can be made using any steamed-pudding mold.

- *1 pound fresh kumquats (3½ cups), plus more to slice for garnish (if kumquats are not available, substitute ⅓ cup orange jam for kumquat marmalade made in step 1)*
- *1½ cups granulated sugar*
- *1 cup dried apricots*
- *¼ cup brandy*
- *1 one-inch piece fresh ginger, peeled, cut in half*
- *Zest of 2 lemons, finely grated*
- *8 tablespoons (1 stick) unsalted butter, plus extra for coating mold*
- *1 cup dark-brown sugar*
- *3 large eggs*
- *½ teaspoon pure vanilla extract*
- *1¾ cups all-purpose flour*
- *2½ teaspoons baking powder*
- *⅛ teaspoon salt*
- *1 cup milk*
- *1 cup crème fraîche or double cream*

1. Slice kumquats into ¼-inch-thick pieces; remove seeds. Combine kumquats and granulated sugar in medium saucepan. Cook slowly over low heat, stirring often with wooden spoon, until the kumquats start to release their juices, 10 to 15 minutes. Continue to cook over low heat, stirring often, until kumquats have softened and liquid has thickened slightly, 25 to 35 minutes. Transfer to small bowl.
2. Combine apricots, brandy, ½ cup water, ginger, and zest of 1 lemon in medium saucepan. Cover; bring to boil over medium-high heat. Reduce to simmer, and cook until almost all liquid has evaporated, 15 to 20 minutes. Remove ginger; discard. Transfer to food processor; purée until smooth; set aside.
3. Butter an 8-to-10-cup pudding mold and a circle of parchment paper that is 4 inches wider in diameter than the mold.

4. In bowl of an electric mixer, cream the butter and brown sugar on medium speed until lightened, 1 to 2 minutes. Beat in the eggs, one at a time, until fully incorporated, 1 to 2 minutes with each addition. Add vanilla and remaining zest. Slowly beat in apricot purée. Sift flour, baking powder, and salt; add to apricot mixture in two additions, alternating each with milk.
5. Spoon about ¾ cup kumquat marmalade into mold, arranging marmalade around sides of mold to follow pattern if there is one; reserve remaining marmalade. Pour in batter. Tap mold sharply down on counter to distribute batter evenly. Cover with parchment, and secure with rubber band; cover with foil. Place lid over foil onto mold. Place rack in stockpot, and set mold, lid-side up, on rack. Pour in boiling water to halfway up side of mold. Cover, and bring to boil over high heat. Reduce to medium low, and steam for 2 hours and 20 minutes. Remove; let sit for 15 minutes. Uncover, and invert mold onto a serving plate; garnish with sliced kumquats, if desired. Serve warm or at room temperature with dollop of crème fraîche or double cream and reserved marmalade on the side.

holiday FRUIT TART

serves 8

1 recipe Pâte Brisée (recipe follows)
1 cup all-purpose flour
¼ teaspoon salt
½ teaspoon ground allspice
½ teaspoon freshly grated nutmeg
½ teaspoon ground cinnamon
1 teaspoon ground ginger
½ cup plus 2 tablespoons dark-brown
*   sugar*
¼ cup currants
¼ cup golden raisins
¼ cup dried cranberries
¼ cup citron
¼ cup candied orange peel, chopped
*   into ¼-inch pieces*
1 cup (4 ounces) finely chopped blanched
*   almonds, toasted*
*   Zest of 1 lemon, finely grated*
2 tablespoons fresh lemon juice
3 tablespoons brandy
¼ cup unsulfured molasses
2 large eggs

1. On a lightly floured surface, roll out three-quarters of the pâte brisée to fit a rectangular 13-by-4-inch tart pan to thickness of ⅛ inch. Place pastry in pan; gently press it down with your fingers into edges and along rim. Trim pastry along edge of pan. Cover with plastic, and refrigerate, along with the remaining dough, while making filling.

2. Sift flour, salt, and spices into bowl. Add sugar, dried fruit, citron, orange peel, almonds, zest, and juice. Stir in brandy, molasses, and 1 beaten egg. Pack into the pastry-lined pan.

3. On a lightly floured surface, roll out remaining dough to ⅛-inch thickness. Moisten edges of pastry in pan with water; place rolled dough over filling. Seal well, and trim away excess dough. Chill in refrigerator for 1 hour.

4. Heat oven to 325°. Cut three slits in tart with a knife to make air vents. Whisk remaining egg with 1 tablespoon water in small bowl. Brush tart with egg wash; place tart in oven. Bake until pastry is golden brown and flaky, about 1 hour and 40 minutes. Let cool on wire rack to room temperature. Using a serrated knife, slice into ¾-inch-thick slices.

PATE *brisée*

makes enough for 1 double-crust
13-by-4-inch tart

2½ cups all-purpose flour
1   teaspoon salt
1   cup (2 sticks) cold, unsalted butter,
*   cut into ½-inch pieces*
*   Ice water (¼ to ½ cup)*

1. Combine flour, salt, and butter in a food processor. Process until mixture resembles coarse meal, about 8 seconds. Add ice water drop by drop through feed tube with machine running, just until dough holds together.

2. Turn dough out onto a large piece of plastic wrap. Press dough down into disk with your hands. Wrap in plastic, and chill in the refrigerator for at least 1 hour; soften before using.

BELOW: **This spiraling steamed pudding (right) gained its formidable stature from a mold Martha found at a tag sale, but any steamed-pudding mold can be used for the recipe. The pudding's batter is flavored with a lemony purée of dried apricots; kumquat marmalade lines the mold before baking. Portions of the pudding will be topped with dollops of crème fraîche (left). A sweet tart filled with dried fruit, candied citrus peel, and almonds (front) is served in slices.**

FLOWERS & GREENERY

What would Christmas be without the tree? Without wreaths, garlands, poinsettias? Imagine the holiday without them—it would lose much of its beauty, fragrance, and whimsy. Flowers and greenery set the stage for the season's celebration.

Once the tree is in its stand and decorated, and the wreath is hanging on the front door, it feels like Christmas—but there's still more to do. Evergreen garlands can be swagged across the mantel, doorways, windows, and mirrors; they can be wrapped around table legs, banisters, and porch railings. Bring wreaths indoors; hang them on the wall, loop a tiny one around a doorknob, place one on the table as a centerpiece.

Flowers can be used to embellish garlands, or on their own. Poinsettias, the most traditional Christmas bloom, don't have to be quite so traditional; look for miniature varieties, as well as pink, yellow, and white ones. And just because it's Christmas doesn't mean you can't use other fresh flowers as well. Almost anything can be used in holiday arrangements; who says a Christmas centerpiece can't be purple? Use the flowers that you love most—as you would for any occasion. To give a bouquet extra holiday cheer, tuck holly or bright-red berries among the flowers.

Find new places in your home for greenery and flowers. Make an arrangement for your bedside table, and you'll wake up feeling merry. Have a Christmas tree in every room of the house: Decorate small live evergreens with just a few ornaments or lights, then plant them outdoors in the spring. Fill your home with life and color for the holidays—and don't forget the mistletoe.

ABOVE: A traditional evergreen garland draped across a window is anchored at the corners with pinecone rosettes and finished with pinecone "tassels." PREVIOUS PAGES, LEFT AND RIGHT: A holiday garland begins with a laurel base and is decorated with pomegranates, rose hips, garden roses, and fragrant white *Cyrtanthus* lilies. Red anemones massed together in a silver bowl are striking in their simplicity and display the beauty of using nontraditional flowers in holiday arrangements; stems are cut to the same length so, when placed in the bowl, the blooms form a dense dome.

RIBBON MEDALLION Embellish an indoor garland or wreath with a red paper medallion (*above*). The pleated center is made from wired paper ribbon; it has thin wire running along the edges, so it can be formed into various shapes. The outer "ribbons" can be made from any medium-weight paper. Start by pleating wired paper ribbon (the length depends on the size you want the medallion to be), and curve it into a circle. Use craft glue to join the ends. Use a longer piece of wired paper ribbon to make a second circle that's a little larger. Glue them together with dabs of glue. For the paper ribbons, cut a wide strip of paper with pinking shears; bend in half without creasing; glue ends together. Repeat, making a total of eight ribbons in two different sizes. Glue ribbons together in pairs, with ends flush. Glue pairs to the back of pleated rings. For the solid-paper center, cut out a circle with pinking shears; fold it in half, then in half again several more times. Unfold and glue into center. To hang the medallion as shown, cut a round of heavy paper or cardboard smaller than the outer ring. Bend a piece of green floral wire (about eighteen inches long) in half, and insert ends through the round of paper about an inch apart from one another. Glue round to back of medallion so wire ends are loose. Position medallion on garland, and wrap the wire ends around the garland; twist wires to secure.

PINECONE ROSETTE Create a more dramatic effect with pinecones and evergreens by anchoring a garland with a spiky cluster of pinecones (*right*). Start by cutting a three-inch Styrofoam ball in half. Cut or tear brown tissue paper into strips. Use a paintbrush to coat half of the foam ball with craft glue, and then smooth on strips of tissue paper, until it is covered completely. Cut floral wire into pieces six to eight inches long. Wrap the center of one piece of wire around the base of one pinecone, and twist the wire to secure, leaving the ends loose. Attach the pinecone to the Styrofoam by poking the wire ends through it and out the flat side; twist and fold the wire flat to secure. Continue adding pinecones, working from the edge to the top of the dome, until the entire dome is covered; leave the flat side bare. To add a wire loop for hanging, bend another piece of wire in half and poke the ends through the Styrofoam near the edge and out the back; instead of pulling the wire all the way through, leave a loop at the edge. Twist the wire ends together, and fold them against the flat side. Or, send one long wire through Styrofoam, perpendicular to the flat edge, leaving six to twelve inches of wire on either side. Position the cluster on the garland or swag, and wrap the wire ends around it. Hang the garland or swag with the pinecone clusters at the corners.

ABOVE: **Small evergreens add to the holiday fragrances indoors, and once the weather warms up, they can be planted outside. During their stay in the house, hide the roots in an attractive bucket or pot, and decorate the trees with lights and ornaments—and don't forget to water them.**

The Christmas tree takes a prominent spot in your home and serves as a focal point of the holiday season; here are some suggestions for choosing a good one, caring for it, and recycling it at the end of the season.

TREE FARMS From an environmental point of view, there is nothing wrong with cutting down Christmas trees. These trees are grown on farms like any other agricultural product, so it's no more destructive to buy a Christmas tree than a head of lettuce. Tree farms are usually established on land that can't support other crops. According to the National Christmas Tree Association, for every Christmas tree that is cut and sold, two to three are planted in its place.

Christmas-tree farms not only discourage the removal of evergreens from forest land; they also contribute to the ecology of the region in which they are located, as they generate oxygen and provide a habitat for birds.

For more information, you can contact the National Christmas Tree Association (see the Guide), which can refer you to your local association for a list of tree farms and lots.

CHOOSING A TREE When you cut your own tree at a tree farm, you know you're getting a fresh one. At a cut-tree lot, however, it helps to know what to look for.

A fresh tree should still have bright-green needles. Gently squeeze a few of them in your hand; a fresh evergreen aroma is a good sign. Carefully bend back a handful of needles; if they snap or break in temperatures above 20 degrees, move on to the next tree. If the tree is a manageable size, bounce its base firmly on the ground; the tree shouldn't drop a lot of needles. Finally, take a look at the base of a cut tree for drops of resin, or sap, which indicate that it has been freshly cut.

CARING FOR A CUT TREE Before you put your tree in its stand, use a handsaw to cut a quarter inch from its base; this allows the tree to drink in water. Use a tree stand that holds at least one gallon of water; if your

stand doesn't, you'll need to check on it more frequently to make sure it always contains water. If you're not putting the tree up immediately, still cut its base, and stand it in a five-gallon bucket of water in the basement or an unheated garage.

Keep the decorated tree away from sources of heat and drafts, such as fireplaces and radiators. Place it a few feet away from the doors and windows that face south or west. Always turn off the tree lights before going to bed.

SMALL LIVING TREES After the holidays, a living tree can become a permanent part of the landscape. With its roots swaddled in burlap, a small evergreen can wait out the winter in a bucket; layer pinecones around the trunk to hide the burlap and to protect the roots. The tree can stay indoors for up to ten days; water and mist it daily to keep it from drying out. Then move it somewhere cool, like a porch or garage, until the ground thaws and the tree can be planted.

RECYCLING PROGRAMS Many communities across the country have started recycling programs for Christmas trees. The most common method of recycling trees is to shred them into mulch. Some towns on the ocean use the trees to stabilize sand dunes and protect the shore from erosion. Trees can also be tied together, weighted, and sunk into reservoirs to create habitats for fish.

In some cities, there are drop-off sites where residents deposit Christmas trees, which are then recycled. Larger urban centers often have curbside pickups of trees. In New York City, for example, trees are collected every January and turned into mulch, which is distributed to community gardens, parks, and playgrounds. To find out how to recycle your Christmas tree, call your local sanitation or environmental department. Remember to remove everything from the tree—including lights, ornaments, stand, garland, tinsel, and plastic bags—before donating it.

RECYCLING IN THE GARDEN You may want to recycle your Christmas tree yourself for the garden. Branches can be clipped and placed over perennial beds as a wintertime mulch. Crisscross branches two layers thick to let air in but keep light out. In the spring, when first sprouts appear, remove boughs in two stages, about four days apart. Use narrow trunks for bean poles or tomato stakes.

If your community does not recycle trees, it might be worthwhile to rent a tree shredder with your neighbors to make mulch.

You may want to observe a tradition from the Middle Ages, when the tree was moved outside as a shelter for birds. Decorate the tree with strings of popcorn and cranberries, bird seed, corn stalks, and sunflower heads.

Whatever you do, don't burn your Christmas tree immediately after the holidays. The tree will be too moist to burn properly and will let off creosote, a coal tar, into the atmosphere. To use your tree as firewood, cut it into small logs, and let them stand for a year.

ABOVE, LEFT TO RIGHT: Christmas trees are cultivated on farms, and environmentalists agree that buying one does no damage to the earth. After the holidays, a Christmas tree can even be put to good use in the garden. Martha begins by sawing off the tree branches. Then she layers the branches on perennial beds for protection during the winter. Smaller branches serve the same purpose on planted urns; tie branches into place.

ROSE AND BERRY TREE This Victorian-style arrangement in the shape of a Christmas tree *(opposite)* has been updated by Michael and Lisa George, florists based in New York City. Built on a base of florist's foam, the arrangement is made with 'Porcelino' roses and *Hypericum* berries. You can use the same technique with different flowers for the tree shape, and you can choose any seasonal berries, sprigs of greenery, pearl-tipped pins, small glass balls, or other decorations for the accents. An arrangement like this can be made in almost any vase or bowl with sides that are at least four inches high. **(1)** Begin by using a knife to shave a piece of florist's foam into the shape you need. It should fill the vase you're using and extend above the top of the vase to a point three inches below the height you want the arrangement to be. Wet the foam first to make it easier to carve. Place the foam into the container. **(2)** Clean the rose stems of foliage, and cut each stem to a length of four inches. Starting at the rim of the vase, insert the stems into the florist's foam horizontally, circling the foam as shown. After making one or two concentric circles, insert a single rose at the top of the foam; this determines the arrangement's overall height. Hold a straightedge so it extends from the top rose to the bottom circle of roses; this will show you the line you want to follow to complete the conical tree shape. Continue adding roses in circles from the bottom; hold the straightedge up to the arrangement as necessary to maintain the shape. If the roses you're using are very tight, leave a little room between them to allow them to open. If the roses are already open, cluster them closer together. **(3)** As you near the top, begin inserting the stems at an angle, then vertically. If necessary, cut the last few stems shorter. **(4)** After you've created the entire tree shape, tuck *Hypericum* berries or some other decorations among the roses. For the tree to stay fresh, it should be watered from the top as often as necessary to keep the florist's foam damp.

POMEGRANATE AND FLOWER GARLAND Fresh pomegranates, rose hips, garden roses, and fragrant white *Cyrtanthus* lilies are wired onto a laurel base in this garland being made by Lisa and Michael George *(left)*. The finished garland is shown on page 24. Other greenery, such as pine or balsam, can be used for the base; other fruits, berries, and flowers can be used to decorate it. Miniature apples and pears would be lovely additions. Start by making clusters of flowers or berries—or flowers *and* berries—by wrapping floral wire around their stems; wire that comes on a paddle is easiest to work with. After making several clusters, begin wiring them into the garland. Wrap the wire around one end of the garland to secure it, then lay a cluster of flowers onto the garland, and wrap the wire around the stems and the garland a few times. Without cutting the wire, add another cluster, and wire it into place. Continue, adding flowers and berries along the length of the garland. Fruits can be wired in as you go, or attached afterward with precut lengths of wire wrapped around their stems *(below left)*.

ROSE, HOLLY, AND BERRY ARRANGEMENT Classic Christmas colors come together in an elegant arrangement of 'White Bianca' roses, holly, and *Hypericum* berries *(opposite)*. It is made following the same technique used for the rose and berry tree on page 31, but the shape is modified into a low dome. Use a knife to shave florist's foam so it fits into the bowl or compote of your choice, extending just above the rim; if you wet the foam first, it will be easier to carve. Clean rose stems of foliage, and cut so they're three to four inches long. Starting near the bowl's rim, insert the stem ends into the foam, making a circle of roses all the way around. Next, insert one rose at the top, determining the height of the arrangement. Continue adding roses from the bottom, in concentric circles; use the height of top rose as a guide for positioning the roses around the sides. Trim stems if they need to be shorter. Tuck holly and berries between roses. Water arrangement as necessary to keep the florist's foam damp.

POINSETTIAS

In a season filled with greenery, poinsettias provides brilliant bursts of color. *Euphorbia pulcherrima*—the poinsettia's official name—is not merely the most popular Christmas plant; it is also the number-one potted flowering plant in America today, in wholesale dollar volume. According to U.S. Department of Agriculture figures, almost seventy million poinsettias are grown in the United States each year.

HISTORY The poinsettia's history is as colorful as its leaves. According to folk legend, a penniless Mexican girl who had no gift for the baby Jesus was forced to resort to picking a bunch of roadside weeds. Her spontaneous bouquet of poinsettia branches, the story goes, suddenly burst into brilliance.

A far more reliable tale, however, is that of a German immigrant's son named Paul Ecke. When the Ecke family arrived in Southern California around the turn of the century, they began growing fields of poinsettias to harvest as cut flowers, selling bouquets along Sunset Boulevard. By the 1960s, the operation was moved indoors, and the climate could be controlled. Under the tutelage of the Eckes and a handful of other breeders, the palette extended to include pink, peach, yellow, and white.

CHOOSING A POINSETTIA To get the freshest poinsettia, select a plant with tight cyathia, the tiny beadlike yellow or green flowers clustered at the center of the red leaves. The red leaves, which we perceive as petals, are actually called bracts. The stems themselves should be stiff, with rich green leaves all the way down. The bracts should be fully colored, not tinged green at the edges—a sign the plant was rushed to market.

CARING FOR POINSETTIAS Keep the plants at 65 to 70 degrees (they may die below 50 degrees), out of drafts, and away from heat sources. A poinsettia requires six to eight hours of sun daily, though direct midday light can fade the bracts. Water when the

soil surface is dry to the touch, keeping it moist, but not soggy; never let water stand in the saucer. By March or April, when the bracts go a muddy green, cut the plant down to a height of eight inches. Let it grow in a sunny window or outdoors all summer, and feed it twice monthly, potting up to a larger container around June.

As next Christmas approaches, how do you turn your green plant red again? The poinsettia is photoperiodic, which means that it responds to lengthening nights. It must have fourteen hours a night of total, absolute darkness from October 1 onward to be red in time for the holidays. Placing the plant under a large box at night or stashing it in a darkened room might work. But even a moment of light will confuse the plant.

ABOVE: 'Lilo Pink,' grown as a mini single-stem plant, reaches five to seven inches in height. OPPOSITE: Tree-shaped poinsettias, known as 'Grande Topiaries,' in an Ecke Ranch greenhouse in Encinitas, California, where about 90 percent of the world's poinsettias get their start.

Though red is still the most popular color, poinsettias can be pink, peach, yellow, or white. New varieties continue to be developed as breeders try to come up with easy-to-grow plants with longer-lasting color. The ones above are trademarked and bear the first name Eckespoint. TOP ROW: Creamy-pink 'Parfait' has delicately crinkled bracts (the large leaves that simulate petals). 'Lemon Drop,' an early bloomer, flowers around Thanksgiving. 'Jingle Bells' has red bracts flecked with pink. SECOND ROW: 'Angelika Marble' is pink with creamy white marbled accents. 'Freedom Pink,' one of the newer pink varieties, was bred to hold its color a long time. 'Pink Peppermint' is pinkish peach and lightly speckled. THIRD ROW: The flowers on 'Pink Curly' plants form compact rosettes. 'Monet' is an unusual cultivar with multicolored bracts, varying from light to dark. Medium-height 'Angelika White' has full branches.

PINECONE WREATH Silvered pinecones can be made into an elegant, sparkling wreath *(right)*. You'll need a double-wire wreath form in the diameter of your choice, pinecones, silver spray paint, and thin silver wire (twenty-gauge works well). Working in a well-ventilated area, spray-paint the pinecones silver. Let them dry thoroughly. Cut an 8-to-10-inch length of wire for each pinecone. Wrap the end of a piece of wire around the base of each pinecone. Create clusters of pinecones by twisting the wires of two or three pinecones together; the number of pinecones in each cluster depends on their sizes and shapes. Attach one cluster to the wreath form by wrapping the wires around the form; to make it more secure, weave the pinecones' wires between the two wires of the form. If you find that the wires on the pinecones are longer than you need, trim them down. Continue adding clusters of pinecones until the form is filled. If there are any gaps among the clusters, fill them by wiring in single smaller pinecones. If you wish, decorate the wreath with a big red bow.

BERRY WREATH Use seasonal berries for a dramatic red wreath. These are hawthorn berries *(right)*, but you can use whatever is abundant in your area; using a mix of berries gives wonderful variation in color and shape. The only supplies you need are berries on their stems, a double-wire wreath form in whatever size you wish, and green floral wire, preferably on a paddle, which is easiest to work with. Wrap the end of the floral wire around the wreath form. Gather several berry stems together, and lay them on the form where the wire is attached. Wrap the wire around the end of the stems and the wreath form about three times, joining them together tightly. Do not cut the wire. Lay another bundle of berries on the form so it overlaps the first one by half, and wire it in place. Continue adding bundles of berries until the entire form is covered. To finish, cut the wire, and wrap it securely around the form.

GARLANDS & ORNAMENTS

How can you choose a favorite ornament? There are expensive ornaments and dime-store ornaments, old ornaments and new ornaments, whimsical ornaments and elegant ornaments. Each and every one is capable of conjuring vivid memories.

Handmade ornaments, though, are particularly special—they have sentimental value even before they've spent a season on the tree. In this chapter, you'll learn how to transform craft-store supplies, such as paper, aluminum, tinsel, and paper clay, into beautiful, lasting ornaments and garlands. You can even let your little elves help—many of these projects are well-suited to children.

Shimmering silver decorations can be fashioned out of thirty-six-gauge aluminum foil. Aluminum holly leaves make bright, unconventional garlands. Wired tinsel is easily formed into sparkling icicles to be suspended from your evergreen's branches. And paper is a remarkably versatile medium, fit for even the most formal tree. There are paper snowmen, stars, spheres, and abstract shapes to hang on a tree. With an old-fashioned technique called quilling, strips of paper curl into intricate snowflakes. Victorian-style paper cones filled with pastel candies are hung from the tree with ribbon. The simplest paper chain makes a charming garland.

Traditional German molded cookies called springerle have a new resilience when made from paper clay instead of dough, which may crumble over time. But real cookies also make great ornaments, as proven by our gingerbread and lacy royal-icing snowflakes.

A collection of ornaments should never stop growing. All of these, whether you make a few of them or a multitude, will feel like old favorites by next year. If you think you don't have room for them, think again: You can always get a bigger tree.

ABOVE: Aluminum ornaments become garlands when strung onto ribbon, hung on wire, hot-glued onto wire, or attached to plain wire swagged with crinkle wire. PREVIOUS PAGES, LEFT AND RIGHT: A Christmas tree decorated exclusively with handmade silver and white ornaments. Elegant aluminum oak leaf garlands drape a mantel and antique mirror.

ALUMINUM LEAF GARLAND Aluminum leaf garlands are crisp companions to evergreen boughs. The leaves, as well as other decorations shown in this chapter, are made from thirty-six-gauge aluminum foil, available from craft stores. It is sturdy enough to hold its shape, but thin enough to work with easily. You can cut it with scissors, but it will dull the blades; use an old pair, or try tin snips instead. **(1)** Draw a leaf shape, with a stem, on paper; then trace the shape with a dull pencil onto the aluminum foil. Scratch veins onto each leaf with your fingernail. Cut out the shape. **(2)** Twist the stem of a leaf around twenty-gauge wire; continue adding the leaves, alternating placement on either side of the wire. Once the stems are fastened, use a hot-glue gun to apply a dot of hot glue to the center of the back of each leaf; tack them into place so they lie flat.

PAPER SNOWFLAKE Start by folding a square or rectangle of paper into accordion pleats. The number of pleats determines the number of points on the ornament: Four pleats will equal eight points, for example. Fold the accordion of paper in half to find the center; staple it, once at the center, perpendicular to the folds. If your ornament is too long for your stapler, you can fashion a staple out of wire; insert the wire through two small holes in the center, and twist together at the back. Make cuts in the folded paper; the corners you cut off (forming the points) should be the flaps of paper, not the folds. The more cuts you make, the more intricate the design; different angles will give entirely different looks. Experiment with plain paper before working with fancier stock. Fan the sides out so they meet, and secure on the back with small pieces of tape. Use Scotch Magic tape, which is easier to remove at the end of the season, so you can store these ornaments flat. **(3)** Hang ornament from pretty thread or other thin string.

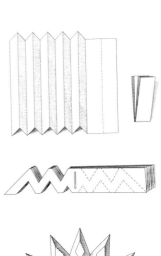

PAPER SNOWFLAKE

EMBOSSED ALUMINUM ORNAMENTS An embosser prints a raised pattern on all kinds of paper and aluminum foil. It costs more than other tools used for these ornaments ($30 to $60, depending on the intricacy and size of the design), but can be a wise investment for making multiple ornaments. You can buy embossers with various designs or have one made to your own specifications by providing a design on a piece of paper (drawn freehand, taken from a clip-art book, or created on a computer) to a vendor. Embossers are sold at art-supply and craft stores. **(1)** Place a sheet of thirty-six-gauge foil into the embosser, squeeze, and release. Cut out the pattern with scissors, tin snips, or pinking shears. **(2)** To give an ornament a tarnished finish, rub it gently with a piece of extrafine steel wool. Then brush surface with a few drops of aluminum blackener (a liquid that will create an instant patina), leave it for a few seconds, and wipe it off with a cloth. Rub steel wool across the ornament once more to even out the color. Punch holes in the ornaments with an ⅛-inch hole punch, and attach hooks, cord, or wire to hang them from the tree. **(3)** String ornaments and glass-bead spacers together for another sparkling decoration for the tree. **(4)** To make a garland of crinkle wire and ornaments, start by threading a piece of plain wire through a strand of crinkle wire. Use jewelry pliers to wrap the short pieces of wire or hooks onto the plain wire and crinkle wire, and then attach the ornaments and the beads, spacing them several inches apart.

HAND-DRAWN ALUMINUM ORNAMENTS To make a variety of ornaments, draw designs freehand with a scribe **(5)**—a pointed jeweler's tool—or a nail. It will be much cheaper than buying assorted embossers. Use a pen or dull pencil to sketch the shape of an ornament onto a piece of cardboard, and cut it out. Trace around cardboard template onto foil with a scribe or nail, cut out shape with scissors or tin snips, and carve the patterns directly onto the foil.

OPPOSITE: Delicate aluminum leaf garlands, foil ornaments, and an array of vintage glass balls give this tree a somewhat formal style.

PAPER STAR This decoration *(below)* is made using the same technique as the paper snowflake (see page 41 for instructions), but make the cuts in the paper as shown. Use any plain or fancy paper you wish.

PAPER TASSEL A tassel is the perfect finish for a simple paper chain *(right)*. The tassel can be made in any size. Use a utility knife to make evenly spaced cuts along a piece of paper as shown. For a bicolored tassel, prepare two different colored papers. Roll the papers up tightly, and glue at the top to secure. Make a loop out of a short band of paper; glue it to the uncut end of the tassel, where it will join the tassel to the paper chain. Glue a band of paper around the top of the tassel. To form the strips into the bell shape, loosely roll them with a pen or other round object into the tapered shape.

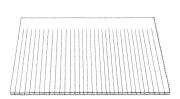

PAPER STAR

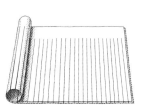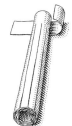

PAPER TASSEL

ABOVE: With silver paper, a little greenery, and a few flowers, a sitting room takes on a festive appearance. Handmade paper stars and tassels put the finishing touches on the paper-chain swag across the mantel. Topiaries, holly branches tucked behind the mirror, and cut amaryllis add Christmas color and spirit.

PAPER CONES Materials for making cones include **(1)** decorative paper, wire, silver beads, and wired tinsel. Wired tinsel has been used for more than a century by glass-ornament makers. It can be ordered by the yard from Christmas or craft catalogs. (It can also be used to make the icicles shown on the tree on page 38: Spiral ten-inch pieces of tinsel around a small tapered rod—paint-brush handles work well. Hang icicles from tips of Christmas tree branches.) **(2)** Cut paper into a 3-, 4-, or 5-inch square; lay it face down on a flat surface. Place compass point at one corner of the square; extend its arm to an adjacent corner. Drag the pencil across the square to form an arc; cut along line with scissors or a utility knife. **(3)** Wrap resulting fan-shaped piece of paper together to form a cone; glue edges together with a thin coat of clear-drying glue. Use a paper clip to hold the seam together while the glue dries. Decorate the top with silver rickrack, wired tinsel, or other fancy trim. Cut a length of trim long enough to fit around top of cone; glue it onto the inside or outside of rim, beginning at the seam. (Position the rickrack halfway inside the rim so it has a scalloped effect from the outside.) **(4)** To fasten a bead at the point of the cone, pull a threaded needle (with thread knotted at end) through bead and the hole in bottom of cone until bead is positioned snugly at the point. Pull string taut inside the cone, tape string to inside wall, and trim. To attach a handle, punch holes with an ⅛-inch hole punch in opposite sides of the cone, approximately ⅜ inch from rim. String ribbon or beaded wire through holes. Secure ribbon ends with knots; curl wire ends.

RIGHT: Filling cones with sweets, like these pastel candies, makes them into wonderful little gifts or party favors. OPPOSITE: Icy paper cones, brimming with colored candies, are a modern version of the Victorian English ones, which were filled with fruits and nuts. Made from patterned and textured paper, they are trimmed with rickrack and vintage silver tassels and hung with ribbons and beaded wire.

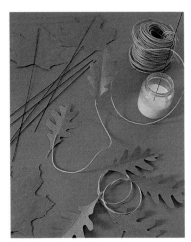

OPPOSITE: A wreath woven with flowers and red pepperberries encircles a light in the hall; three ribbons are tied to the wreath, then knotted to the top of the light chain. In the dining room, fresh bay leaves follow the lines of the chandelier without getting too close to the candles.

PAPER WREATH This wreath *(above)* is the ideal complement to a tree filled with paper ornaments—and is also lovely on its own. Trace a leaf or draw one freehand; use that design as a template to cut lots of leaves out of various shades of green paper. Cut a 12-inch single-wire wreath form, and bend the form into a horseshoe shape; bend the two ends back ½ inch to form small hooks for hanging. Glue a 12-inch length of twenty-gauge floral wire, available precut at craft stores, onto the back of each leaf *(left)*. Starting at the top of one side of the form, attach a leaf by wrapping its wire stem around the form. Continue adding leaves, overlapping them by about half, until you reach the center. Repeat, covering the other side with leaves. Bend leaves on their stems into just the arrangement you want. Add a big red bow in the center. Hang the wreath from small nails or hooks, or with fishing line.

CHAIR SWAG An evergreen decoration on the back of each chair *(above)* makes the holiday dining room more festive and fragrant. The swags can be made from any sprigs of greenery, giving you the chance to put to good use the leftovers from a wreath or garland. The version shown above includes a few pepperberries; be warned, however, that if you use berries, they could stain carpets and upholstery. Begin by wiring the pieces of greenery together at the top. Cut a piece of ribbon to the length you want for each decoration. For an upholstered chair, tack the ribbon at its midpoint to the back of the chair using a twist pin (a pin with a flat plastic head and corkscrew-style stem, made for upholstery). Hold the bundle of greenery against the ribbon, and tie the ribbon around it. For openwork wooden chairs, tie the ribbon onto the chair back; then tie the greenery in place.

PAPER-CLAY ORNAMENTS To make these crisp, white ornaments (*left*), molds are filled with paper clay—a lightweight, durable substance sold at craft stores. **(1)** The rectangular molds are springerle forms, the numbers are vintage architectural molds, and the others are chocolate molds. **(2)** Roll clay flat, at least ½ inch thick, on waxed paper. Spray molds lightly with cooking spray; wipe off excess. Press springerle molds onto clay; remove. Cut around imprint with a dough scraper or metal spatula. For larger molds, pack a ¼-inch-thick layer of clay into mold; remove. To make an eye hook, cut beading wire about 1½ inches long; bend it in half. Grasp curved end with pliers; twist loose ends to form a loop. Clip the frayed end to make a clean edge; pierce it into top of ornament while clay is wet. Eye screws, available at hardware stores, also work. **(3)** Use needle-nose pliers to shape beading wire into hooks for hanging and to make small segments adorned with glass beads or ribbon bows. When the ornaments are dry, smooth edges with fine-grained sandpaper.

QUILLED SNOWFLAKE To make the snowflake (*opposite*), you'll need a quilling needle (or a toothpick) and quilling paper, which can be bought in precut widths and a vast assortment of colors. Each snowflake requires eight strips of quilling paper, each ⅜ inch wide and 4½ inches long; the ornament itself is about 2½ inches tall. Before working on the ornament, practice some quilling basics. Wind a strip of paper around the needle to form a tight curl. Play with the paper to stretch it out to the shape you want. Try folding a strip in half and curling both ends inward for a heart shape. For the snowflake, fold each strip so that one of the halves is about ½ inch longer than the other, and curl the ends to make the piece as shown. Repeat with seven more strips. On a flat surface, fit the pieces together with their points in the center. Using tiny dabs of glue, attach pieces together in pairs, then join the four pairs. Let glue dry, and attach a piece of metallic thread to hang ornament.

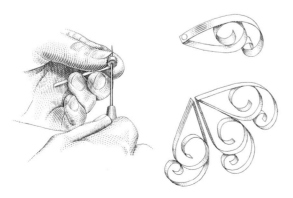

QUILLED SNOWFLAKE

ABOVE: **Folded paper stars, paper strip spheres, and antique glass ornaments trim a "tree" of laurel branches atop a handsome demilune table. The bare winter branches are wired together and secured in a painted cast-iron urn filled with florist's foam; a soft covering of sheet moss finishes the arrangement.**

52 CHRISTMAS WITH MARTHA STEWART LIVING

STRIP SPHERES To make these ornaments, you will need quilling paper and an awl **(1)**. Cut a piece of wire about an inch longer than you want the sphere **(2)** to be. Then cut strips of quilling paper the appropriate length; each strip goes all around the ornament. For 4-inch-tall spheres, we used 12-inch strips of paper; use eight or ten strips for each sphere. Use a tack or an awl to make three holes in each of the strips: one in the center and one ¼ inch from each end. Insert one end of the wire into the center hole of one strip; bring ends of strip around, and hook over other end of wire. Repeat, alternating colors. Use round-nose pliers to turn wire ends into small loops. Adjust strips for an even sphere. To make a tassel for the bottom of sphere, see page 44.

SNOWMAN WITH TOP HAT The snowman **(3)** is a slightly more complicated version of the strip sphere. For this one, we used eight 8-inch strips of ¼-inch quilling paper and a 6-inch wire; each strip of paper is curved around the wire in an S shape. Make a hole at each end of each strip of paper, and make one hole off-center (4½ inches from one end). Insert the wire though the hole at the end of each strip of paper; start at the end farther from the off-center hole so the bottom sphere will be the bigger one. After all eight pieces have been threaded onto the bottom of the wire, use pliers to turn that wire end into a small loop. One at a time, push the threaded end of each strip up from the bottom a little, allowing you to insert the top of the wire through the off-center holes. Finish the S shape by hooking the last hole of each strip over the exposed wire. Adjust the paper loops to make two spheres, leaving some exposed wire at the top for the snow-

man's hat. The hat is made from four pieces of quilling paper, 4¼ inches long. Make a hole in the center of each strip. Mark and measure the four folds you'll make in each strip: The first fold should be ¾ inch from one end, then 1 inch from there, then ¾ inch, then 1 inch, leaving ¾ inch at other end. Fold on these lines as shown, and insert each hole in the top of the exposed wire. Glue a band around to keep the hat intact. Loop the top of the wire with pliers.

SEWN SILHOUETTE We used decorative paper with a different color on each side for these **(4)**, but you can use any medium-weight paper. Stack three or four sheets (ours were 3½ by 5 inches), fold them in half, and run them through the sewing machine, stitching along fold. Leave long threads at one end to use for hanging ornament. Fold in half along seam, and draw silhouette of any shape, as shown; the threads should be at the top. Cut out along outline, and fan papers out. Knot ends of the thread, and hang the ornament.

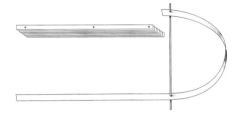

STRIP SPHERES

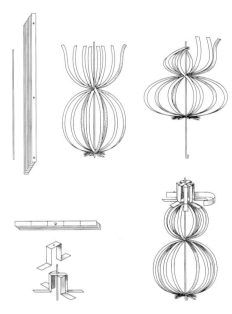

SNOWMAN WITH TOP HAT

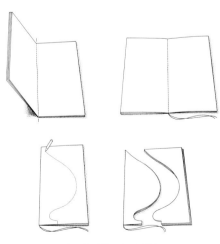

SEWN SILHOUETTE

ROYAL-ICING SNOWFLAKES These ornaments *(left)* are dramatic against a lush evergreen. **(1)** Start by drawing a simple or an intricate snowflake on paper (or photocopy one of the templates on page 132). The design should be 2 to 5 inches across. Lay a piece of waxed paper over design, and secure papers to work surface with tape. Fit a pastry bag with a plain round tip (#4 to #7; the thicker the lines, the sturdier the ornament will be), and fill with royal icing (see recipe below). Pipe royal icing onto waxed paper, following the lines. Make continuous lines of icing, instead of stopping and starting. If you wish, embellish with dragées (these small silver-colored balls are for decorative use only). **(2)** Pour granulated sugar over, covering whole snowflake. **(3)** Untape papers, hold over a bowl, and tap off the excess sugar. Let snowflake dry thoroughly, at least 8 hours. Slowly and carefully peel waxed paper off snowflake; it will be very fragile. Turn it over so the flat side is facing up, and pipe more icing over each line of snowflake; minor breaks can now be repaired. Add dragées, and dust lightly with sugar. Let dry again, 8 more hours. When completely dry, use ribbon or cord to hang from the tree.

royal ICING

makes about 2 cups

2 large egg whites
1 pound confectioners' sugar

Using an electric mixer on low speed, beat the egg whites, 2 teaspoons water, and confectioners' sugar for about 10 minutes. If the icing is too thick, add an additional teaspoon of water; if the icing is too thin, continue beating it for 2 to 3 minutes to achieve a thicker consistency. Note: Raw eggs should not be used in food prepared for pregnant women, babies, young children, the elderly, or anyone whose health is compromised. Five tablespoons meringue powder, mixed with a scant ½ cup water, may be substituted for the egg whites.

makes about 16 large cookies

6   *cups sifted all-purpose flour*
1   *teaspoon baking soda*
½   *teaspoon baking powder*
1   *cup (2 sticks) unsalted butter*
1   *cup dark-brown sugar, firmly packed*
4   *teaspoons ground ginger*
4   *teaspoons ground cinnamon*
1½ *teaspoons ground cloves*
1   *teaspoon finely ground black pepper*
1½ *teaspoons salt*
2   *large eggs*
1   *cup unsulfured molasses*
    Silver dragées (for decorative use only)

1. In a large bowl, sift together flour, baking soda, and baking powder. Set aside.
2. In bowl of an electric mixer, cream butter and sugar until fluffy. Mix in spices and salt, then eggs and molasses. Add flour mixture; combine on low speed. Divide dough into thirds; wrap in plastic. Chill at least 1 hour.
3. Heat oven to 350°. On a floured work surface, roll dough to ⅛-inch thickness. Cut out cookie shapes. Transfer to ungreased baking sheets, and refrigerate until firm, about 15 minutes. Bake for 8 to 10 minutes, or until crisp but not darkened. Let cookies cool on wire racks, then decorate as desired.

GINGERBREAD SNOWFLAKES These classic gingerbread cookies (see recipe at right) are delightful, whether you hang them on the tree or serve them to holiday visitors. The dough should be rolled out to a thickness of ⅛ inch—the cookies need to be thin so they won't weigh down tree branches. If you're making oversize cookies, use two spatulas to transfer the dough to the baking sheet. Or cut dough directly on the baking sheet, and remove excess dough before lifting the cutter. **(1)** If you're planning to hang the cookies on the tree, bend a piece of pretty cord—silver is a good choice—into a loop, and lay the ends into a dot of royal icing (recipe opposite) on the back of the baked, cooled cookie; apply a generous amount of icing over the cord. Let dry for about 8 hours. **(2)** To decorate the cookies, fit a pastry bag with a #2 or other small round tip, and fill with royal icing. Pipe the icing onto the baked, cooled cookies in different snowflake patterns. While icing is still wet, decorate with dragées if you wish. Let the icing dry thoroughly, about 8 hours.

ABOVE: An abundance of royal-icing, gingerbread, and paper ornaments fills a spectacular Christmas tree; the presents beneath the tree carry out the pink-and-white color scheme.

COLLECTING ANTIQUE ORNAMENTS Everyone knows that Christmas ornaments are rich in sentimental value, but when they're antiques, they can also have quite a bit of monetary value—early ornaments are now prized and expensive.

The classic ball was first made in nine-teenth-century Germany by glassmakers. Kugels, meaning "hollow balls," were silvered inside—perfect for hanging on a tree, since they reflected the glow of candlelight.

During the 1860s, German immigrants brought Kugels to America, and in the 1880s F.W. Woolworth began importing them. In 1890 alone he bought and sold two hundred thousand Kugels; before he gave up his importing business in 1939, he had sold at least $25 million worth of glass ornaments. Today, prices of Kugels range from a few dollars to more than $1,000, depending on condition, color, and style.

Dresdens, intricate silvered and gilded cardboard ornaments, also from Germany, are much harder to find and pricier than Kugels; prices start at about $50, and rise astronomically. Three-dimensional Dresdens often held candy and were discarded when empty; flat ones were more likely to be pre-served, usually in Victorian scrapbooks.

Ornaments from the 1930s to the 1960s don't have as fine a pedigree, but they do come with a much lower price tag. A cotton pear from the 1930s will cost about $10; Czechoslovakian beaded ornaments of the same vintage can sell for $5 apiece. Ornaments from the 1960s can be found for even less.

Some modern manufacturers are using vintage molds and methods, so it pays to know how to recognize authentic pieces. Newer glass ornaments are lighter, and the colors more garish. They also lack the fine detail that makes antique ornaments real works of art. Many collectors claim you can date glass ornaments by the style of the cap, but this method isn't always reliable, since an ornament and its original cap are often separated. Some replacement caps are newer and some older, so a collector must also learn to recognize the heft and patina of an antique piece.

ABOVE: Glass fruits like these were ornaments of the poor in the Victorian era, while the wealthy hung real fruit. OPPOSITE, CLOCKWISE FROM TOP LEFT: Glass birds from Germany, circa 1920. Tiny wire baskets, like these German ones from the early 1900s, held candy. To make glass figural ornaments like these 1930s Santas, craftsmen carved a shape from wood or clay and cast a mold. A fish—a symbol for Christ, the "fisher of men"—was a common motif. Egg-shaped Kugels, ridged orbs, and grape clusters were all popular; pears are rare; all of these date from the 1890s, except for the red, ridged ornament, made in Japan in the 1920s or 1930s. Many ornaments made in America during World War II have little or no paint and use waxed cardboard and string caps rather than metal. CENTER: Large, heavy Kugels were frequently hung over doorways or in windows.

HANGING ORNAMENTS There's a safer, more secure way to hang ornaments than with the standard sharp hooks. Cut green floral wire into four-to-six-inch pieces. String one end of wire through the ornament's hanger, and twist it tight around the other half of the wire. Position the ornament just beneath the branch you want to hang it from, and twist the wire around the branch several times. At the end of the season, you can leave the wires on ornaments, unless they're antique or valuable, in which case wires should be removed.

STORING ORNAMENTS Wrap your ornaments individually in acid-free tissue paper, and pack them into sturdy containers, preferably compartmentalized ones. Look for boxes with dividers at discount and housewares stores as Christmas approaches. Never wash antique ornaments; just dust them gently with a soft brush. Ornaments should be stored in a dry spot; in most houses, this rules out the basement and the attic, which experience extremes of temperature and humidity.

TAKING DOWN THE TREE At the end of the season, just removing the ornaments invites an avalanche of needles. But there are ways to get the tree out of the house and keep the mess to a minimum. One tidy method is to use a tree bag, a big plastic bag that goes under the tree, hidden beneath a tree skirt—but you need to remember to do it when you're putting the tree up. When it's time to take the tree down, just lift the bag up, encasing the tree, and take the whole thing outside. Look for tree bags at hardware stores during the Christmas season. You can also wrap the tree in a sheet to move it outside. Or, you can leave the tree in its place, clip off the branches, carry them out in plastic bags, and sweep up the mess—which will be contained in one spot. For information on recycling your Christmas tree, see page 29.

ABOVE: A box of ornaments from the 1930s includes a cardboard-and-glitter star from Germany and house from Japan, as well as a sailboat and diamond, both made of handblown beads in Czechoslovakia. OPPOSITE, TOP ROW: The German blown-glass basket (far left) holds paper flowers; the faces of the paper angels are pasted on; the blown-glass baubles (center) are wrapped with crimped wire; the tinsel snowflake is made from real gold and copper. SECOND ROW: Gilded and silvered cardboard Dresdens, from 1870 to 1900, may have been handed out as party favors. THIRD ROW: Real and glass pinecones, nuts, and berries were often hung on the tree. BOTTOM ROW: In the 1920s and 1930s, legions of snowmen were produced from glass, cotton, cardboard, and plastic.

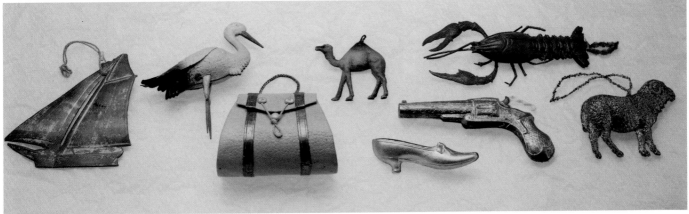

MERINGUE

White as snow and light as a cloud, meringue is a dream dessert for the holidays. It is dramatic and delicious—without a trace of fat. Even the process of creating meringue is miraculous, as egg whites and sugar are transformed into soft, sloping peaks.

Once you understand the science behind meringue, making it is surprisingly easy. Unlike other liquids, egg whites stay foamy once air has been beaten into them because a group of proteins called albumin reinforces the bubble walls. And meringue stands up to baking because one of these proteins, ovalbumin, helps keep the meringue from cracking. Nothing must interfere with the work of the albumin. Even a speck of egg yolk will decrease the volume of the foam by as much as two-thirds. Since fat clings to the surface of plastic bowls even after washing, bakers use bowls made of glass or metal, especially copper, which has a stabilizing effect on egg foams. Another stabilizer is acid, usually in the form of a trace amount of cream of tartar, which lowers the pH of the albumin and helps prevent overbeating.

The next concern is how long to beat the egg whites. Whip them with a whisk or an electric mixer, beginning on low speed. They will turn white and smooth as you gradually increase the speed. Stop beating when the foam is stiff enough to stand up in peaks. In fact, you should be able to turn the bowl upside down without disturbing the foam. If the foam turns lumpy, you'll know you have beaten too long and must start again with new whites.

Most of the recipes on the following pages use Swiss meringue, which can be piped into cookies in whimsical shapes or can be used as a topping, filling, or a crisp tart shell. However you choose to serve meringue, it will look heavenly and taste divine.

ABOVE: Boxes made of piped Swiss meringue are ideal for the busy holiday season, as they can be made a few weeks in advance. PREVIOUS PAGES, LEFT AND RIGHT: Holiday desserts include meringue porcupines, baked Alaska, baked meringue apples, and a variety of cookies. A meringue box makes an exquisite holder for scoops of sorbet.

swiss MERINGUE

makes 4 cups

Swiss meringue is best for piping into shapes that are to be baked until crisp.

4 large egg whites, at room temperature
1 cup sugar
Pinch cream of tartar
½ teaspoon pure vanilla extract

1. Fill medium saucepan one-quarter full with water. Set the saucepan over medium heat, and bring water to a simmer.
2. Combine egg whites, sugar, and cream of tartar in the heatproof bowl of electric mixer, and place over saucepan. Whisk constantly until sugar is dissolved and whites are warm to the touch, 3 to 3½ minutes. Test by rubbing between your fingers.
3. Transfer bowl to electric mixer; whip, starting on low, gradually increasing to high until stiff, glossy peaks form, about 10 minutes. Add vanilla; mix until combined. Use meringue according to recipes that follow.

simple MERINGUE

makes 7 to 8 cups

This meringue is used for the Pavlova (page 68).

6 egg whites, at room temperature
1 teaspoon freshly squeezed lemon juice
½ teaspoon pure vanilla extract
1½ cups superfine sugar
1½ tablespoons cornstarch

1. Combine egg whites, lemon juice, and vanilla in electric mixer. Whip, first on low speed, then slowly progressing to high speed, until soft peaks form, about 1½ minutes.
2. Slowly sprinkle the sugar a little at a time over the egg-white mixture, and whip until glossy peaks are formed, about 3 minutes.
3. Sift the cornstarch over the meringue, and fold in. Use meringue immediately.

meringue BOXES *with* SORBET

makes 3 boxes

These boxes are easier to make than they look—and fun, too. Almost any piping style will produce a beautiful box (see page 73 for technique). Your creations will keep for a few weeks if stored in an airtight container at room temperature.

1 recipe Swiss Meringue
2 pints sorbet, any flavor

1. Heat oven to 200°. Use a pencil to trace six 3-inch squares and twelve 2-by-3-inch rectangles on a piece of parchment paper. Place paper, penciled-side down, on baking sheet.
2. Reserve 1½ cups of the meringue for later use. Fill a pastry bag, fitted with a coupler, with meringue, and attach a tip of your choice. Pipe out the meringue in desired patterns within the penciled squares and rectangles. The piped lines or designs should connect, but you should leave plenty of open spaces in between the piping. Cover remaining meringue with plastic, and set aside.
3. Bake piped meringue for 15 minutes. Reduce the heat to 175°, and bake for an additional 35 minutes or longer, until the meringue is dried but still white. Watch carefully; lower heat if meringue browns.
4. Return the remaining meringue to bowl of an electric mixer, and rewhip until light, fluffy, and glossy. Fill a pastry bag, fitted with a plain tip, with the meringue. On a parchment-lined baking sheet, assemble the boxes by piping the meringue along edges of bottom square and piping meringue between side rectangles. Change the tips, and pipe out a decorative pattern on the outside joints to hide your work. Do not attach the top of box.
5. Return the baking sheet to the oven, and bake until the second piping of meringue is hard and dry, about 45 minutes. Remove from oven, and let cool completely.
6. Scoop the sorbet into each box, and serve with the top to the side or placed over sorbet.

BELOW: A perfectly beaten meringue will hold its shape beautifully, as demonstrated by these graceful peaks. Depending on how it is baked, the meringue may remain pure white or become tipped with golden brown.

chocolate-meringue COOKIES

makes 30 cookies

¼ cup cocoa powder, plus 2 teaspoons
    more for dusting

1 recipe Swiss Meringue

1. Heat oven to 175°. Line a baking sheet with parchment paper.
2. Sift ¼ cup of the cocoa over the meringue, and fold so that streaks of cocoa remain.
3. Fill a pastry bag fitted with a tip of your choice (we used an Ateco #5 star tip); pipe out cookies in small coils or desired shapes onto baking sheet. Sift remaining cocoa over cookies; bake 2 hours, until cookies lift off parchment easily.

almond-meringue SANDWICHES

makes 2 dozen sandwiches

5   egg whites

¼   teaspoon cream of tartar

1   cup superfine sugar

1½   cups blanched ground almonds

½   cup heavy cream

6½   ounces semisweet chocolate, finely
     chopped

1. Heat oven to 200°. Line two baking sheets with parchment paper.
2. Combine egg whites and cream of tartar in the bowl of an electric mixer. Whip on medium speed until soft peaks form. Gradually add sugar, 1 tablespoon at a time, beating until whites are shiny and firm, about 3 minutes. Fold in ground almonds.
3. Fill a pastry bag fitted with Ateco #864 star tip with meringue. Pipe out 2-inch-round cookies onto prepared baking sheets.
4. Place in the oven, and bake until the meringues just start to color, about 15 minutes. Turn off the oven, and let the meringues cool for 4 hours or overnight. For a quicker method, reduce the heat after 15 minutes to 175°, and cook for 1½ hours. Remove from oven, and let cool completely.
5. Meanwhile, scald cream in a small sauce-pan. Place chocolate in a medium mixing

bowl, and pour hot cream over chocolate. Whisk until chocolate is smooth and melted. Let cool completely. Fill a pastry bag with chocolate filling, and pipe out onto half the cookies—the bottom sandwich halves. Make sandwiches with remaining cookies, and serve. Sandwiches can be stored in airtight containers for 2 to 3 days.

ABOVE: A pale-pink Christmas cookie was piped with a leaf tip to resemble a poinsettia. OPPOSITE: This festive assortment of cookies began with a single batch of Swiss meringue; shapes were piped from a pastry bag using various tips. Meringue can be tinted with paste or gel food colorings, or flavored with cocoa powder or nuts.

lime-meringue TART

serves 12

Use a nonreactive saucepan (stainless steel or enamel, but not aluminum) when making citrus curds; otherwise, the curd may discolor and pick up a metallic taste.

- 4 large egg yolks
- 2 large eggs
- ¾ cup sugar
- ½ cup freshly squeezed lime juice (about 4 limes)
  Zest of 2 limes
- 4 tablespoons unsalted butter, cut into small pieces
- 1½ recipes Swiss Meringue

1. Whisk together egg yolks and eggs. Combine with sugar and lime juice in small saucepan. Cook over medium-low heat, stirring constantly, 8 to 10 minutes, or until mixture is thick enough to coat back of spoon.
2. Stir to cool slightly. Strain into small bowl; add butter, a piece at a time, stirring until smooth. Stir in zest; let cool completely. Cover with plastic; refrigerate until needed.
3. Heat oven to 200°. Trace three 6-inch circles on parchment; place, penciled-side down, on a 12-by-18-inch baking sheet.
4. Fill a clean pastry bag, fitted with Ateco #12 plain tip, with the meringue, reserving about 1½ cups; pipe out meringue, starting in center of each circle, spiraling out to circle's edge (see page 72 for technique). Create 1-inch-tall wall of meringue peaks by piping along outside of circle using same tip to create smooth peaks, or change tips for a more decorative edge. If making bite-size tarts, follow the same spiraling process on sixteen 2-inch circles, creating ¾-inch walls.
5. Place the baking sheets in the oven, and bake about 20 minutes. Reduce the heat to 175°, and bake 40 to 60 minutes more, until the meringue is dry and crisp, but still white. Let stand to cool completely on baking sheets. The shells can be packed in airtight containers and stored for several weeks.
6. Heat oven to 475°. Fill cool meringue tarts with chilled lime curd. Rewhip remaining

meringue on high speed until stiff, about 5 minutes. Fill pastry bag fitted with Ateco #5 star tip; pipe a ring of decorative peaks on top of lime curd. Bake until lightly browned, about 2 minutes. Serve immediately.

meringue PORCUPINES
with cream FILLING

makes 12 sandwiches

The spiky look of these cookies is the reason they got their name.

1   recipe Swiss Meringue
½   cup heavy cream
2   drops pure almond extract
1   cup plus 2 tablespoons best-quality
    peach or apricot preserves

1. Heat oven to 400°. Line two baking sheets with parchment paper.
2. Scoop spoonful of meringue onto large oval soupspoon, and use another soupspoon to form meringue into shape of small egg. Use second spoon to push meringue oval off first spoon and onto parchment. Spoon 12 ovals onto each prepared baking sheet. Using a small offset or icing spatula, pull out spikes of meringue, creating a porcupine effect (see page 73 for technique).
3. Reduce oven to 200°; bake meringues until they are crisp on the outside but have a marshmallow consistency on the inside, about 1 hour. Reduce oven to 175° if meringues start to brown. Remove from oven, and gently press bottom of each meringue so it caves in and can be filled. Turn off oven, and return meringues to oven to dry, about 20 minutes. Let meringues cool completely before filling.
4. Combine the cream and almond extract in chilled bowl of an electric mixer, and whip on medium speed, just until stiff, about 2 minutes. Fill half the hollowed meringues with cream mixture, the remaining half with preserves, and sandwich together. Serve as soon as possible after filling.

ABOVE: Irresistible, prickly-looking meringue porcupines can be eaten individually or, as shown here, sandwiched around a luscious filling of fruit preserves and almond-flavored whipped cream.

ABOVE: **Pavlova, a meringue shell filled with whipped cream and fruit, was named after Anna Pavlova, the Russian ballerina; the dessert was invented in 1926 by an Australian chef to honor the dancer's visit to his country. A sprig of mint and bright red raspberries, strawberries, and red currants make the colors and flavor of Pavlova the perfect finale to a special holiday dinner.**

PAVLOVA *with fresh* RED FRUITS

serves 6

For this Christmas dessert, look for the best berries available. Consider mixing in some preserved lingonberries or chunky strawberry preserves if the fruits aren't very juicy.

1 recipe Simple Meringue
2 pints total of fresh red fruits, such as red currants, raspberries, strawberries, and a few pomegranate seeds
¼ cup kirsch or Grand Marnier
¼ cup granulated sugar
½ pint heavy cream
Mint sprigs, for garnish
Confectioners' sugar, for dusting

1. Heat oven to 400°. Line two baking sheets with parchment paper.

2. Using a rubber spatula, spoon three to four 1-cup blobs of meringue onto each prepared baking sheet, leaving 3 inches of space between each blob. Lift up sides of each blob with a small offset spatula, and flip meringue back across the top, creating six to eight smoothly folded pillowlike squares (see page 72 for technique).

3. Reduce oven temperature to 200°. Place baking sheets in oven; bake until meringues are crisp on outside but have a marshmallow consistency on inside, about 1½ to 2 hours. Check by poking into bottom of a pillow. Reduce temperature to 175° if meringues start to brown. Remove from oven, and let cool completely on a rack.

4. Meanwhile, combine the fruit, liqueur, and ¼ cup granulated sugar in a mixing bowl. Let stand, gently stirring once or twice, about 1 hour or longer, depending on the fruits, until soft and juicy.

5. Pour cream into chilled bowl of electric mixer, and whip, on medium speed, until cream is just stiff. Break pillows open, and place each on a dessert plate. Fill open pillows with whipped cream, and top with berries. Garnish with mint sprigs and a dusting of confectioners' sugar.

baked meringue APPLES

serves 6

You will get the best results if you use one of the apple varieties listed here. Microwaving cooks the apple shells quickly and preserves their color.

10 *Cortland, Jonathan, or Granny Smith apples (about 4 pounds)*
1 *lemon*
¼ *cup sugar, plus 1 tablespoon for sprinkling*
2 *tablespoons unsalted butter*
2 *tablespoons brandy or cognac*
½ *recipe Swiss Meringue*
1 *recipe Caramel Sauce (recipe follows)*

1. Core six apples by cutting a cone from the top of each with a paring knife. With a melon baller, scoop out seeds down to the bottom. Juice the lemon into cavity of each apple, and sprinkle each apple with ½ teaspoon sugar. Place three of these apples on a microwave-safe plate, and loosely cover with plastic wrap. Microwave on high power until the apples are translucent and cooked through, but not caving in, about 3½ to 4 minutes. Remove from the microwave, and repeat with the three remaining cored apples. This cooking time will vary from oven to oven, so turn apples occasionally, and check the window periodically. The apples will bubble up with juices when almost done.

2. Heat oven to 450°. Peel, core, and slice the remaining four apples into ¼-inch-thick wedges. Melt the butter in a large saucepan over high heat. Add the apple wedges, and toss to coat. Sauté for about 1 minute, and sprinkle ¼ cup of sugar over the apples. Sauté, tossing often, until the apples are brown and translucent. Carefully add the brandy (it may ignite), and toss again.

3. Transfer microwaved apples to a baking sheet, and stuff with the sautéed apples. Set aside in a warm place.

4. Fill a pastry bag, fitted with Ateco #5 star or any other large star tip, with meringue.

Pipe meringue onto each apple in decorative swirls. Place in the oven, and bake until meringue just starts to brown, 1 to 2 minutes. Remove from oven, and serve warm with Caramel Sauce.

caramel SAUCE

makes 1 cup

¾ *cup boiling water*
1 *cup sugar*
    Dash pure vanilla extract
1 *teaspoon cognac*

Combine ¼ cup boiling water and sugar in a medium saucepan. Cook on high until caramel forms, about 5 minutes. Remove from heat, and slowly whisk in remaining ½ cup water at arm's length, being careful not to splatter hot caramel. Remove from heat, and stir in vanilla and cognac.

ABOVE: Whole baked apples are stuffed with sautéed apple slices that have been spiked with brandy. The meringue topping is piped with a large star tip; baked for just a minute or two, the peaks brown at the tips but remain soft. The homey dessert is served with a caramel sauce.

ABOVE: Slicing into this baked Alaska reveals its rich layers of pistachio ice cream, berry sorbet, cherry ice cream, and chocolate cake beneath the covering of meringue. OPPOSITE: After being completely assembled, here with a combination of pistachio and cherry ice creams, this classic American dessert is baked briefly in a very hot oven; as the igloo-like shell browns, the ice cream remains insulated from the heat.

baked ALASKA

serves 6 to 8

This old-fashioned dessert has become popular again, and why not? An ice-cream cake covered with an igloo of meringue emerging from an oven is a real showstopper.

> 6   *tablespoons sugar*
> 3   *egg yolks*
> 1   *teaspoon pure vanilla extract*
> 3   *ounces bittersweet chocolate, melted and cooled*
> 3   *egg whites, at room temperature*
>   *Pinch of salt*
> 1½ *pints pistachio ice cream, slightly softened*
> 1½ *pints cherry ice cream or berry sorbet, slightly softened*
> 1   *recipe Swiss Meringue*
>   *Vegetable-oil cooking spray*

1. Heat oven to 350°. Line an 8-inch cake pan with parchment paper, and spray with cooking spray.

2. Combine 3 tablespoons sugar and yolks in bowl of an electric mixer; whisk, on medium speed, until pale yellow and thick, about 15 minutes. Add vanilla, and fold in melted chocolate just to combine.

3. Combine the egg whites and pinch of salt in bowl of electric mixer; whip, on medium speed, until frothy. Add remaining 3 table-spoons sugar; beat until stiff. Fold the egg whites into the chocolate mixture.

4. Carefully pour batter out onto prepared cake pan. Bake until cake is set and top is dull, about 20 minutes. Remove from oven, and let cool on a wire rack.

5. Spray a 5-cup-capacity metal bowl with nonstick cooking spray; line with plastic. Pack base of bowl with pistachio ice cream; layer cherry ice cream over pistachio, then finish with another layer of pistachio ice cream (or layer ice creams and sorbets as you desire). Pack firmly, cover surface with plastic wrap, and place in freezer. Freeze until ice cream is very hard, at least 2 hours or up to 24 hours in advance.

6. Place cake on parchment-lined baking sheet. Remove ice cream from the freezer, and invert bowl over cake. Keep the ice cream covered with plastic wrap, and return ice-cream cake to the freezer.

7. Heat oven to 500°. Fill a pastry bag, fitted with Ateco #5 star tip, with meringue; pipe onto ice cream in a decorative fashion, or spoon meringue over ice cream and swirl with a rubber spatula. If ice cream starts to soften, return cake to freezer for 15 minutes.

8. Place in oven, and bake until meringue just starts to brown, 1 to 2 minutes. Remove from oven, and serve immediately.

COOKIES Swiss meringue is firm enough to be piped into a variety of shapes using standard pastry tips, such as star, leaf, petal, and round tips. Meringue can be mixed with nuts or cocoa powder, or with food coloring. To add color, dab in small amounts of food-coloring pastes or gels (do not use powders or liquids) with a toothpick. Any additions should be gently folded in after the meringue has been whipped so you don't interfere with the foaming process. To bake these cookies, heat oven to 200°. Pipe or spoon meringue onto parchment-lined baking sheets, and bake about 20 minutes; reduce heat to 175° and bake for 40 to 60 minutes more, until cookies are dry and crisp but not browned.

TART SHELLS This basic meringue tart shell can hold a variety of fillings. With a pencil, draw a circle on parchment paper (this one is 6 inches in diameter; tart shells can be any size). Turn paper over and place on a baking sheet. Using a plain round pastry tip, pipe a spiral from the center out **(1)**; keep piping in one continuous line until circle is filled. Use any pastry tip to pipe a decorative border of small peaks around the edge of the tart shell **(2)**. Bake until meringue is dry and crisp, but still white (see recipe on page 66). Remove from oven; let cool completely. Fill tart shell. If desired, pipe meringue peaks on top of filling and bake until soft meringue peaks are lightly browned.

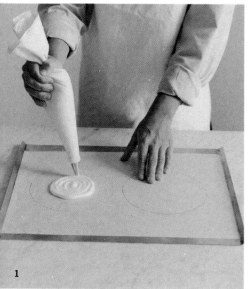
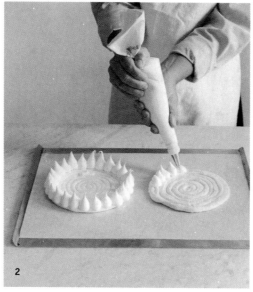

PILLOWS The Pavlova with fresh red fruits and whipped cream begins with meringue "pillows." Line a baking sheet with parchment paper. Spoon about one cup of simple meringue onto the parchment **(3)**. Using a small offset spatula, lift one side of the meringue, and flip it back over the top in a single motion. Repeat on remaining three sides **(4)**, so the meringue looks like a folded, pillowlike square. Bake until the pillow is crisp on the outside, with a soft and chewy consistency on the inside (see recipe on page 68).

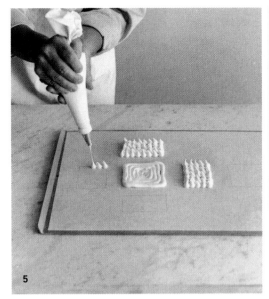

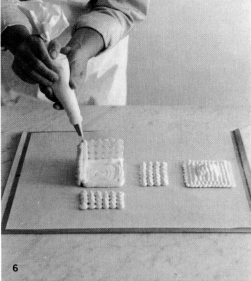

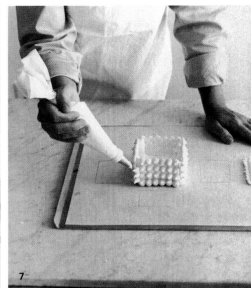

MERINGUE BOXES Line a baking sheet with parchment paper. With a pencil, draw two 3-by-3-inch squares (for top and bottom of box) onto parchment, then draw four 2-by-3-inch rectangles (for sides). Turn parchment paper over. Fill a pastry bag, fitted with a coupler, with meringue, and attach the pastry tip of your choice. Each square can be piped in any design **(5)**. For bottom of box, use a plain round pastry tip. For sides, use any tip you like; star, leaf, petal, and round tips all give good results. When creating the design, make sure piping is connected but does not completely overlap; you want to create lacy openings. Bake until dried (see recipe on page 63). Remove from oven; let cool completely. Assemble the box by piping meringue along edges of bottom square and piping meringue between side rectangles **(6)**. On outside of box, hide seams with decorative piping **(7)**. Bake again according to recipe.

PORCUPINES This dessert starts with an oval, known in culinary terms as a quenelle. When decorated with tiny spikes, it resembles a porcupine. Eat it plain like a cookie, or as a sandwich, with two quenelles surrounding the filling of your choice. Fill an oval soupspoon generously with meringue. Using a second spoon, pass the meringue from spoon to spoon until the

quenelle shape is smooth **(8)**. Use the first spoon to gently scrape the meringue onto a baking sheet lined with parchment paper. With a small offset spatula, quickly pull out small spikes along quenelle **(9)**. Bake until the meringue is crisp (see recipe on page 67). If you are making porcupine sandwiches, pick up each quenelle carefully after it has been baked, and gently press bottom with your fingers so that it caves in. Let cool completely. Fill the hollowed porcupines, and sandwich together.

COOKIES & CANDIES

Batch after batch of cookies emerging from the oven is a sure sign that Christmas is near. While favorite recipes are always handed down from one generation to the next, there's room for new recipes in any baker's repertoire. The recipes on these pages—for cookies and candies—are all particularly worthy additions. From the simplest drop cookies to delicate, chocolate-tipped cigarettes Russes, from luscious golden caramels to handmade chocolates, they offer an impressive variety.

With the candy recipes, even a novice can create confections that might have come from the fanciest shop. Detailed instructions demystify the process, but here are a few more tips: Read all the way through your recipe twice, and have everything ready before you begin. By the time the sugar syrup is ready to come off the stove, it will be too late to figure out what to do next. Boiling sugar is much hotter than boiling water, so always work attentively. Use the size pot that the recipe suggests—sugar syrup can triple in volume and overflow a small pot; in a pot that's too big, the syrup will spread so thinly across the bottom that it could burn.

When you package cookies and candies as gifts, think beyond the standard tins. Look in kitchenware shops, art-supply stores, and even hardware stores for unusual containers such as bowls, metal cake pans and loaf pans, pudding molds, lunch boxes, and tool boxes. A bow of wide satin ribbon, rickrack, metallic cord, or other festive trim may be all the wrapping they need.

Gifts from the kitchen are always appreciated during the holidays. But don't forget to make plenty of extras for yourself—when it comes to cookies and candies, more is always merrier. And Christmas certainly wouldn't be Christmas without them.

ABOVE: **These raspberry crumb cookies are substantial enough to be served as dessert, with a scoop of vanilla ice cream on the side. PREVIOUS PAGES, LEFT AND RIGHT: Springerle, traditional German ornamental cookies, remain white during baking. Luminescent fruit jellies with flavorful hues; from top: pineapple, rose, fig, cranberry, grape-anise, and apricot.**

ABOVE: **To make springerle, a simple dough with a subtle anise flavor is rolled out on a work surface dusted with confectioners' sugar, a mold is pressed into the dough, and the excess is trimmed away. Springerle originated hundreds of years ago; today, replicas of the traditional European molds are available in more than one hundred designs. The cookies are made with lots of eggs, whose leavening effect may have given them the name** springerle, **which means little jumper in German.** BELOW: **Raspberry crumb cookies are composed like miniature tarts, with layers of buttery, crumbly pastry dough above and below a layer of seedless raspberry jam; fluted pastry cutters serve as baking tins.**

SPRINGERLE

makes 50 to 60

6 large eggs, at room temperature

6 cups sifted confectioners' sugar, plus more for dusting

8 tablespoons (1 stick) unsalted butter, softened

½ teaspoon salt

1¼ teaspoons anise extract

11 cups sifted cake flour

1. In bowl of an electric mixer, use whisk attachment to beat eggs on high speed until very thick and lemon colored, about 12 minutes. Gradually beat in sugar until creamy and smooth.

2. Add butter, 1 tablespoon at a time, beating on high speed, until creamy. Add salt and anise extract; beat to combine.

3. Add 8 cups of flour, 1 cup at a time, mixing on medium-low speed after each addition. Change to paddle attachment; add 2 more cups of flour, 1 cup at a time, mixing on medium-high speed until stiff and well combined.

4. Sprinkle a work surface with remaining cup of flour. Transfer dough to the floured surface; knead by hand until the flour is incorporated, about 5 minutes. Divide the dough into 4 pieces; cover with plastic wrap.

5. Dust a work surface with confectioners' sugar; roll out 1 piece of dough ⅜ inch thick. Press a springerle mold into the dough; lift off. Using a pizza cutter or knife, cut out cookie and slide it onto a parchment-lined baking sheet; repeat, arranging cookies by size, about 1 inch apart. Let stand uncovered for 24 hours. Turn cookies over; let stand 24 more hours, until dry on both sides.

6. Heat oven to 250°. Bake cookies, 1 sheet at a time, until completely dry, about 30 to 45 minutes. They will not take on any color. Transfer to wire racks to cool. Store in airtight containers for 2 to 3 weeks.

raspberry-almond CRUMB COOKIES

makes 22

Pastry cutters are used as molds for these tartlike cookies; butter the pastry cutters well so they will slip off easily after baking.

⅝ cup (1¼ sticks) unsalted butter, at room temperature, plus more for cutters

1½ cups very finely ground blanched almonds (5¼ ounces)

1¾ cups all-purpose flour

¾ cup sugar

¼ teaspoon salt

½ cup plus 2 tablespoons best-quality seedless raspberry jam

1. Heat oven to 350°. Line two baking sheets with parchment paper; set aside. Butter 22 two-inch fluted stainless-steel pastry cutters (or two-inch plain pastry rings, if desired); place them 1 inch apart on baking sheets. In a large bowl, whisk together almonds, flour, sugar, and salt.

2. Use a pastry blender or two knives to cut butter into dry ingredients until crumbly, then work with your fingers until there are no dry crumbs. Squeeze mixture, making pieces ranging from pea-size to 1 inch.

3. Place 2 tablespoons of crumb mixture into each pastry cutter. Press crumbs to compress into a ¼-inch-thick layer.

4. Spoon 1¼ teaspoons of jam on dough in each pastry cutter; spread jam to within ⅛ inch of the edge. Sprinkle 2 tablespoons of crumb mixture over jam. Bake 15 minutes, rotate sheets between oven shelves, and bake about 15 minutes more, until cookies are golden brown.

5. Transfer sheets to wire rack. Immediately lift off pastry rings; let cookies stand to cool completely. Store in an airtight container for up to 1 week.

molasses DROP COOKIES

makes 2 dozen

½   *cup (1 stick) unsalted butter*

½   *cup packed dark-brown sugar*

1   *large egg*

¼   *cup plus 2 tablespoons molasses*

1¼   *cups all-purpose flour*

½   *teaspoon baking soda*

¼   *teaspoon salt*

    Granulated sugar, for sprinkling

1. Heat oven to 375°. Line two baking sheets with parchment paper; set aside. In an electric mixer, use the paddle to combine the butter and the brown sugar; mix on high speed until fluffy, about 2 minutes.

2. Add egg and molasses, and mix on medium speed until combined, about 20 seconds, scraping down the sides of the bowl once.

3. In a medium bowl, whisk together flour, baking soda, and salt; add to butter mixture. Mix on low speed to combine, 20 seconds.

4. Using two spoons, drop 2 teaspoons of batter on a baking sheet; repeat, spacing drops 3 inches apart. Bake for 5 minutes. Sprinkle tops of cookies with granulated sugar, rotate sheets between oven shelves, and bake 8 minutes more. Rotate sheets again, and bake about 6 minutes more, until cookies are just brown around the edges. Slide parchment with cookies onto a wire rack; let cool for 15 minutes. Store in an airtight container for up to 1 week.

lemon-ginger DROP COOKIES

makes 3 dozen

½   *cup (1 stick) unsalted butter*

¾   *cup plus 2 tablespoons sugar, plus more for sprinkling*

1   *large egg*

1   *tablespoon grated lemon zest*

1⅓   *cups all-purpose flour*

½   *teaspoon ground ginger*

½   *teaspoon baking soda*

¼   *teaspoon salt*

¼   *cup diced (⅛ inch) crystallized ginger*

1. Heat oven to 350°. Line two baking sheets with parchment paper; set aside. In an electric mixer, use paddle to mix butter and sugar on medium-high speed until light and fluffy, about 5 minutes, scraping down sides of bowl twice. Add egg; combine on high speed. Add zest; mix.

2. In a bowl, whisk together flour, ground ginger, baking soda, salt, and crystallized ginger; add to butter mixture; mix on medium-low speed to combine, 20 seconds.

3. Using two spoons, drop about 2 teaspoons of batter on baking sheet; repeat, spacing drops 3 inches apart. Bake for 7 minutes. Sprinkle cookies with sugar, rotate sheets between oven shelves, and bake until just golden, about 7 minutes more. Slide the parchment with cookies onto a wire rack; let cool 15 minutes. Store in an airtight container for up to 1 week.

BELOW: Clear plastic boxes show off the contrasting colors of these drop cookies. The chewy lemon-ginger cookies and the crisp molasses cookies are both simple to make.

ABOVE: A tempting clutch of cigarettes Russes—light, crisp cookies rolled into tubes and then tipped with chocolate—is encircled by a piece of unfinished wood veneer tied in place with waxed linen string. RIGHT: The cookies are soft when they come out of the oven and must be rolled quickly into shape around a dowel before they have a chance to harden.

CIGARETTES *russes*

makes 35 to 40

Make these delicate wafers one baking sheet at a time so you can roll them while warm.

    2   cups confectioners' sugar, sifted
   1¼   cups all-purpose flour
    ⅛   teaspoon salt
  10½   tablespoons unsalted butter, melted,
           plus 4 tablespoons unsalted butter
    6   large egg whites, lightly beaten
    1   tablespoon heavy cream
    1   teaspoon pure vanilla extract
    4   ounces bittersweet chocolate, chopped
           medium fine
   1½   teaspoons corn syrup
        Vegetable-oil cooking spray

1. In a mixing bowl, combine sugar, flour, and salt; make a well in the center. Add the melted butter, egg whites, cream, and vanilla. Mix until well combined. Refrigerate, covered, for at least 2 hours or overnight.

2. Heat oven to 425°; place rack in center. Spray two baking sheets (do not use air-cushioned sheets or line with parchment) with vegetable-oil spray. Spoon a heaping tablespoon of batter onto baking sheet. Using the back of a spoon, spread batter into a very thin 6-by-3½-inch oval. Repeat, making three more ovals of batter on the sheet.

3. Bake just until brown at edges, about 6 minutes. Meanwhile, prepare second sheet. Working quickly, use a knife or a long metal spatula to transfer a cookie to a work surface; roll around a chopstick or thin wooden dowel, forming a 6-inch cigarette shape; cool on wire rack. Repeat with remaining cookies. If they get too stiff, return baking sheet to oven for 30 seconds. Continue baking and shaping cookies until batter is used up.

4. Combine chocolate, corn syrup, and the remaining 4 tablespoons butter in double boiler over simmering water; stir occasionally with a rubber spatula until smooth. Let cool slightly. Dip 1 inch of each cooled cookie into chocolate. Dry on wire rack, with dipped section off the edge. Store between waxed paper in an airtight container for 2 to 3 days.

pecan-cranberry BISCOTTI

makes 2 dozen

1½ cups pecan halves, toasted

1 teaspoon baking powder

2½ cups all-purpose flour

1¼ cups sugar

⅛ teaspoon salt

3 large eggs, plus 2 large yolks

1 teaspoon pure vanilla extract

1 cup dried cranberries

Zest of 1 lemon

1. Heat oven to 350°. Finely chop half the pecans, and leave rest in halves; set aside.

2. In electric mixer, combine baking powder, flour, sugar, and salt. In bowl, beat eggs, yolks, and vanilla. Add to dry ingredients; mix on medium low until sticky dough is formed. Stir in pecans, cranberries, and zest.

3. Turn dough out onto well-floured board; sprinkle with flour; knead slightly. Shape into 9-by-3½-inch logs. Transfer to prepared baking sheet. Bake 25 to 30 minutes, until golden brown. Let cool enough to handle, about 10 minutes. Reduce oven to 275°.

4. On cutting board, slice logs on diagonal into ½-inch-thick pieces. Return pieces cut-side down to sheet. Bake until lightly toasted, about 20 minutes. Turn over; bake 20 minutes, or until slightly dry. Cool on wire rack. Store in airtight container for up to 2 weeks.

double-chocolate BISCOTTI

makes 2 dozen

8 tablespoons (1 stick) unsalted butter

4 ounces bittersweet or semisweet chocolate, finely chopped

½ cup Dutch cocoa

1¾ cups all-purpose flour

1½ teaspoons baking powder

½ teaspoon salt

1 cup sugar

2 large eggs

1 teaspoon pure vanilla extract

1 cup whole shelled pistachio nuts or blanched almonds, lightly toasted

1 cup golden raisins

1. Heat oven to 350°. Melt the butter and chocolate in double boiler set over, but not touching, simmering water. Stir until mixture is smooth.

2. Sift together cocoa, flour, baking powder, and salt. In electric mixer, beat sugar and eggs on medium speed until lightened. Add vanilla. On low speed, add chocolate mixture, then flour mixture. Stir in nuts and raisins. Dough will be soft.

3. Turn the dough out onto a lightly floured work surface. Form two 9-inch-long-by-3½-inch-wide logs of dough on a parchment-lined baking sheet.

4. Bake for 30 minutes, until dough sets. Cool 15 minutes. Reduce oven to 275°. Slice logs on the diagonal into ½-inch pieces; place the pieces cut-side down on baking sheet. Bake 20 minutes. Turn over; bake 20 minutes more, until pieces are slightly dry. Let cool on wire rack. Store in an airtight container for up to 2 weeks.

ABOVE: Crisp Italian biscotti are delicious on their own or dunked in coffee or dessert wine. To give as a gift, package them upright in a café-au-lait bowl, pull cellophane over the top, and secure at the bottom with a ribbon. BELOW: To achieve biscotti's shape, the dough is formed into a log, baked, sliced, and baked again.

swedish ginger COOKIES

makes 3 dozen

¾ cup strained bacon fat

1 cup sugar, plus more for rolling

4 tablespoons dark molasses

1 large egg

2 cups all-purpose flour

¾ teaspoon salt

2 teaspoons baking soda

1 teaspoon ground ginger

1 teaspoon ground cloves

1 teaspoon cinnamon

1. Heat oven to 350°. In the bowl of an electric mixer, cream together bacon fat and sugar. Beat in molasses and egg. Add the remaining ingredients; combine thoroughly.
2. Shape dough into walnut-size balls, roll balls in sugar, and flatten with fingers on ungreased baking sheets. Bake for 10 to 12 minutes, or until cookies are golden brown and cracked on top. Let cool on wire racks. Store in an airtight container, up to 1 week.

easy chocolate STRIPING

You can decorate big batches of plain cookies faster and more easily than you ever expected with this technique.

1. Cut bittersweet or semisweet chocolate into chunks. Place chunks in a resealable plastic freezer bag, seal the bag, and micro-wave on high until the chocolate melts, 30 seconds to 1½ minutes. Chocolate holds its shape as it melts, so check it by carefully touching the bag, not just by looking at it. Let the chocolate stand until it's cool enough to handle. Meanwhile, arrange cookies of your choice on a baking sheet or on parch-ment; the closer together they are, the less chocolate will be wasted.
2. Snip as small a hole as possible in one corner of bag. Drizzle chocolate over cookies in stripes, spirals, zigzags, even initials.
3. Let chocolate set slightly, then transfer the cookies to a serving plate, or refrigerate until ready to serve.

TOP: The secret to these Swedish ginger cookies is the bacon fat, which gives them a smoky flavor that complements the spicy bite of ginger, cloves, and cinnamon. ABOVE: With this easy technique, melted chocolate can be drizzled over baked cookies in any decorative pattern you wish.

fruit JELLIES

makes 85 to 90

2   ounces gelatin (plus 1 more ounce if making Pineapple Jellies)
Fruit flavoring (see recipes below)
4⅓ cups granulated sugar
1   teaspoon citric acid
1   cup superfine or confectioners' sugar
Vegetable-oil cooking spray

1. Spray two 8-inch-square pans with vegetable-oil spray. Prepare flavoring.
2. In 6-quart saucepan, sprinkle gelatin over 2 cups water; let it soften, about 3 minutes. Add granulated sugar and citric acid. Heat slowly over low heat, stirring constantly with a wooden spoon, until sugar dissolves, about 10 minutes. Wash down sides of pan with wet pastry brush to remove any sugar crystals.
3. Increase heat to high; bring to a boil. Reduce heat to medium low; boil, without stirring, 15 minutes. Watch the syrup: If it starts to turn dark tan before the 15 minutes, it is ready. Remove from heat.
4. Let stand for 5 minutes while bubbles dissipate; some white foam will remain. Whisk in flavoring. Without scraping pot, pour evenly into prepared pans. Let stand, uncovered, for 24 hours. Unmold, and cut into 1-inch squares or other desired shapes; roll in superfine or confectioners' sugar.

PINEAPPLE JELLY FLAVORING

8   ounces dried pineapple
1   tablespoon lemon oil

1. Chop pineapple medium fine. Place in a saucepan with 1 cup water; cover. Bring to a boil. Cook over medium-low heat until most of the water has been absorbed, 15 minutes.
2. Transfer to food processor; process until smooth. Transfer to bowl; mix in lemon oil.

GRAPE JELLY FLAVORING

½   cup grape or boysenberry jelly
1   tablespoon anise extract or oil

Mix together jelly and anise extract or oil.

APRICOT JELLY FLAVORING

4   ounces dried apricots
1   tablespoon apricot oil or orange-flower water

1. Chop apricots medium fine, place in a small saucepan, and add 1 cup water. Cover and bring to a boil; reduce heat to medium low and cook, covered, for 10 to 20 minutes, until water has been absorbed.
2. Transfer apricots to a food processor. Process to a fine purée. Transfer to a bowl, and add apricot oil or orange-flower water.

ROSE JELLY FLAVORING

¼   cup red-currant jelly, sieved to remove seeds
1   tablespoon rose water

Whisk together jelly and rose water.

CRANBERRY JELLY FLAVORING

2   cups fresh or frozen cranberries
1   tablespoon orange-flower water
1   cup dried cranberries

1. Place fresh or frozen cranberries and 1 cup water in a saucepan; cover. Bring to a boil, reduce heat to medium low, and cook until water has been absorbed, 10 to 20 minutes.
2. Transfer to a food processor. Process to a fine purée. Transfer to a bowl. Whisk in orange-flower water and dried cranberries.

FIG JELLY FLAVORING

6   ounces dried figs (about 10)
1   cup dry red wine
½   teaspoon freshly ground black pepper
1   tablespoon pure vanilla extract

1. Chop figs medium fine. Place in a small saucepan, add wine and pepper, and cover. Bring to a boil; reduce heat to medium low, and cook for 15 minutes, until most of the water has been absorbed.
2. Transfer to a food processor, and purée. Transfer to a bowl, and stir in vanilla.

TOFFEE

makes about 70 pieces

The pans recommended below are the ideal fit for the toffee; if you use other pans, make sure they are perfectly flat, and pour the toffee to a thickness of an eighth of an inch.

    2   cups (4 sticks) unsalted butter,
        each stick cut into 8 pieces
    ¼   cup light corn syrup
    2½ cups sugar
    1   pound bittersweet chocolate, chopped
        into small pieces
    3   cups pecans, chopped very fine, sieved
        to remove fine powder
        Vegetable-oil cooking spray

1. Spray a 15-by-10-inch baking pan, a 16½-by-11½-inch baking pan, and an 8-inch-square baking pan with vegetable-oil spray. In a heavy 3-quart saucepan, combine butter, ½ cup water, corn syrup, and sugar. Clip on a candy thermometer. Bring to a boil over high heat, stirring with a wooden spoon. Continue stirring until mixture thickens, about 2 minutes. Wash down sides of pan with a pastry brush dipped in water to remove sugar crystals. Reduce heat to low; stop stirring. Let mixture come to a boil.

2. Let boil, without stirring, until temperature reaches 280° (soft-crack stage). This will take from 35 minutes to just over an hour; it is essential that the mixture continues to boil. Remove from heat. Without scraping pot, pour into prepared pans as evenly as possible. If needed, use a spatula to smooth. Let cool at room temperature for 1 hour.

3. After 45 minutes of cooling, melt chocolate in a double boiler over medium-low heat, stirring with a rubber spatula. Pour over toffee; spread with a spatula if necessary. Let cool about 15 minutes. Sprinkle with nuts; lightly press them into chocolate.

4. Let stand at room temperature for 24 hours. Using a large knife, lightly score 1¾-by-2¾-inch rectangles over chocolate. Cut toffee along scored lines; lift pieces out with a spatula. Alternatively, toffee may be broken into shards. Store in an airtight container for 3 to 4 weeks.

ABOVE, LEFT: Toffee squares are encased in glassine envelopes to keep them from sticking together. TOP: Melted bittersweet chocolate is poured over the cooled toffee. ABOVE: The chocolate is encrusted with chopped pecans. This pan of toffee was cut into neat rectangles, but it can be broken into shards instead.

ABOVE: **These corrugated boxes hold a perfect portion of snow-white nougat studded with almonds. Just one batch of nougat yields enough candy for lots of sweet little gifts.**

french almond NOUGAT

makes about 40 pieces

The basis of this candy is a mixture of sugar syrup and egg whites known as mazetta.

For the mazetta:

   2   large egg whites, at room temperature
   ¾   cup light corn syrup
   ½   cup sugar

For the nougat:

   1½ cups light corn syrup
   1½ cups sugar
   4   tablespoons (½ stick) unsalted butter, melted
   1   teaspoon pure vanilla extract
   ¼   teaspoon salt
   3½ cups whole raw almonds (skin on)
       Vegetable-oil cooking spray

1. Begin by making the mazetta: Using an electric mixer, beat egg whites until stiff; set aside. In a 1-quart saucepan, combine corn syrup, ¼ cup water, and sugar. Clip on a candy thermometer. Bring to a boil over high heat, stirring with a wooden spoon, about 5 minutes. Wash down sides of pan with a pastry brush dipped in water to remove any sugar crystals.

2. Cook over medium heat, stirring occasionally, until temperature reaches 240° (soft-ball stage), 15 to 20 minutes. Remove sugar syrup from heat. Beating constantly on medium speed, slowly pour hot syrup into egg whites. Continue beating for 3 to 4 minutes until syrup is incorporated. Use immediately, or cover and refrigerate until ready to make the nougat.

3. Spray an 8-inch-square baking pan with vegetable-oil spray; set aside. Place mazetta in a large bowl; set aside. In a 2-quart saucepan, combine corn syrup and sugar. Clip on candy thermometer. Bring to a boil over high heat, stirring constantly with a wooden spoon, 5 to 10 minutes. Wash down sides of pan with a pastry brush dipped in water to remove any sugar crystals.

4. Over medium-high heat, cook to 280° (soft-crack stage), 12 to 15 minutes, without stirring. If heat is too high it can boil over, so watch carefully. Remove from heat; let stand for 2 minutes. Without scraping pan, pour syrup over mazetta. Working quickly, stir with a wooden spoon until almost smooth. Stir in butter, vanilla, and salt. Mix until butter is incorporated. Stir in nuts. Scrape into prepared pan, and smooth the top; you may spray your hand with vegetable-oil spray and run it over the warm candy to smooth it. Let stand at room temperature, uncovered, until firm, 4 to 6 hours.

5. Spray a large cutting board generously with vegetable-oil spray. Unmold nougat from pan onto sprayed surface. Cut nougat into 3-by-1-by-¾-inch pieces or other desired shapes. Wrap each piece in cellophane or waxed paper.

golden CARAMELS

makes about 150

Caramels should be individually wrapped in cellophane or waxed paper to keep their shape.

4 cups heavy cream
1 cup sweetened condensed milk
4 cups light corn syrup
4 cups sugar
1 teaspoon salt
1 cup (2 sticks) unsalted butter,
*   cut into 16 pieces*
1 tablespoon plus 1 teaspoon pure
*   vanilla extract*
*   Vegetable-oil cooking spray*

1. Spray an 11¾-by-16½-inch baking pan (this is a half-sheet pan) with vegetable-oil spray. Set aside in a spot where it will not be moved. In a 2-quart saucepan, combine cream and sweetened condensed milk; set aside.

2. In a heavy 6-to-8-quart saucepan, combine corn syrup, 1 cup water, sugar, and salt. Clip on candy thermometer. Over high heat, cook until sugar is dissolved, stirring with a wooden spoon, 8 to 12 minutes. Brush down sides of pan with a pastry brush dipped in water to remove any sugar crystals.

3. Stop stirring, reduce heat to medium, and bring to a boil. Cook, without stirring, until temperature reaches 250° (hard-ball stage), 45 to 60 minutes. Meanwhile, cook cream mixture over low heat until it is just warm. Do not boil. When sugar reaches 250°, slowly stir in butter and warmed cream mixture, keeping mixture boiling at all times. Stirring constantly, cook over medium heat until thermometer reaches 244° (firm-ball stage), 55 to 75 minutes. Stir in vanilla. Immediately pour into prepared pan without scraping pot. Let stand uncovered at room temperature for 24 hours without moving.

4. To cut, spray a large cutting board generously with vegetable-oil spray. Unmold caramel from pan onto sprayed surface. Cut into 1-by-1¼-inch pieces or other shapes. Wrap each in cellophane or waxed paper.

dark-chocolate CARAMELS

makes about 150

The better the quality of chocolate used in these caramels, the more delicious the result.

4 cups heavy cream
2½ cups light corn syrup
4½ cups sugar
½ teaspoon salt
1 pound, 2 ounces bittersweet chocolate,
*   chopped in small pieces*
1 cup (2 sticks) unsalted butter,
*   cut into 16 pieces*
*   Vegetable-oil cooking spray*

1. Spray an 11¾-by-16½-inch baking pan (this is a half-sheet pan) with vegetable-oil spray. Set aside in a spot where it will not be moved. In a heavy 4-quart saucepan, combine 2 cups cream, corn syrup, sugar, and salt. Clip on candy thermometer. Bring to a boil over medium heat, stirring occasionally with a wooden spoon, 15 to 20 minutes. Wash down sides of pan with a pastry brush dipped in water to remove any sugar crystals.

2. Cook, stirring constantly, until temperature reaches 220°, 6 to 8 minutes; watch so mixture doesn't boil over. Continue stirring and add chocolate and butter; keep mixture boiling, and slowly add remaining 2 cups cream. Cook, still stirring, until temperature reaches 240° (soft-ball stage), about 60 minutes, keeping mixture at a low boil.

3. Without scraping pot, pour mixture into prepared pan. Let stand uncovered at room temperature for 24 hours without moving.

4. To cut, spray a cutting board with vegetable-oil spray. Unmold caramel onto sprayed surface. Using a large knife, cut into 1-by-1¼-inch pieces or other shapes. Wrap each in cellophane or waxed paper.

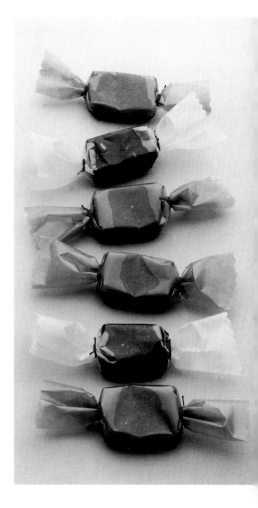

ABOVE: **Classic golden or dark chocolate, these chewy caramels are dense, buttery, and exceptionally rich. Caramels should always be individually wrapped in waxed paper or cellophane as soon as they are cut.**

HANDMADE CHOCOLATES

For a few delightful weeks at the end of each year, we all seem to live in a perpetual state of indulgence and extravagance. And what could be more luxurious than these exquisite handmade chocolates?

People seem to be more passionate about chocolate than about any other food. It's hard to believe that it's been around for less than two centuries. Before that, people drank the mashed paste of the cocoa bean (a dense and bitter substance called chocolate liquor) after whipping it with milk or water and sugar. In 1828, a machine was invented that extracted cocoa butter from chocolate liquor; what remained was a cake of cocoa powder. When the butter was blended with more chocolate liquor, the super-rich result was what we now call baking chocolate. Sugar and vanilla are added to round out the flavor of chocolate used in candy; milk and lecithin are included to make milk chocolate.

Gourmet chocolate—the only kind used to make the confections shown here—begins with beans from the finest trees, blended and roasted for full, rich flavor. It also contains 35 to 50 percent cocoa butter; lesser brands include other fats and fillers. However, cocoa butter is volatile, and chocolate must be precisely tempered to stabilize it in a smooth and silky form. The process involves melting and cooling chocolate to specific temperatures. Chocolate that's not tempered can develop white patches or streaks called bloom. Once you master this single technique (see page 90 for instructions), chocolate becomes a marvelously versatile material.

For many of the chocolates shown here, all you do is fill a mold with tempered chocolate, let it harden, and pop out perfect chocolates. Plastic molds are available in a staggering array of shapes from specialty baking-supply stores and chocolate-making shops. Other techniques include filling chocolate shells with berries, nuts, or ganache, a decadent mixture of chocolate and heavy cream. A chocolate nest and delicate tulip-shaped cups are created by shaping chocolate on the outside of a balloon.

dark-chocolate GANACHE FILLING

makes 1⅔ cups

This soft ganache is specifically for piping into molded chocolates; don't use it to make truffles or other candy. This amount will fill about eighty chocolates.

2 cups heavy cream

17 ounces semisweet chocolate, chopped into very small pieces

1. Heat cream in a medium saucepan over low heat until just about to boil.
2. Place chopped chocolate in a large bowl. Pour hot cream over chocolate, stirring until chocolate is completely melted. Let mixture cool, stirring occasionally. Once ganache is cool it will be quite thick.
3. Beat mixture with paddle attachment of an electric mixer or with a handheld mixer for about 3 minutes, just until it reaches a mousselike consistency; use immediately.

white-chocolate GANACHE FILLING

makes 2 cups

This recipe yields enough ganache to fill about ninety-five chocolates.

2 cups heavy cream

21 ounces white chocolate, chopped into very small pieces

1. Heat cream in a medium saucepan over low heat until just about to boil.
2. Place chopped chocolate in a large bowl. Pour hot cream over chocolate, stirring until chocolate is completely melted. Let mixture cool, stirring occasionally. Once ganache is cool it will be quite thick.
3. Beat mixture with paddle attachment of an electric mixer or with a handheld mixer for about 3 minutes, just until it reaches a mousselike consistency; use immediately.

TOP: Dark-chocolate ganache inside a chocolate shell. ABOVE: Chocolate cups are filled with white-chocolate ganache; the tops are sprinkled with cocoa powder. OPPOSITE: Chocolate cones are simply yet elegantly wrapped in lustrous tinted foils.

LEFT: Geometric chocolates suggest a tempting array of gems and crystals. These were made using a variety of molds; some are patterned, creating stripes and ridges on the finished chocolates; others are plain, resulting in smooth, glossy chocolates. BELOW: Squares of foil protect chocolates from scratches and scuffs. BOTTOM: Precious gems of pure, tempered dark chocolate. OPPOSITE: Dark and white chocolate contrast dramatically on dominoes and card-suit pieces. These are made by piping one kind of chocolate into the indentations in the mold, letting it harden, then filling the mold with the other kind of chocolate.

TEMPERING CHOCOLATE

All chocolate is in temper when you buy it: It breaks cleanly, melts smoothly, and has a gorgeous sheen. But as soon as you melt chocolate, it goes out of temper. That's because cocoa butter is polymorphic, easily assuming different forms. If you don't cool chocolate just so after melting it, you'll wind up with chocolate that's waxy, cakey, or prone to white patches on its surface, or bloom. Peggy Cullen, a New York City confectioner whose company, Lucky Star Sweets, custom-makes chocolates, created the ones shown on these pages. She recommends tempering only quality chocolate. Valrhona, Callebaut, Carma, and Ghirardelli are all good choices. Read the ingredients before you begin; if chocolate contains any additives, fillers, or fats besides cocoa butter, it will not temper.

1. Chop chocolate into bean-size pieces with a chocolate chopper (a metal-tined instrument). One and a half pounds is a good amount to work with at one time; it's enough to make two to four dozen chocolates, depending on size and filling. A smaller amount of chocolate cools too quickly; more becomes unwieldy. In a microwave-safe plastic bowl, heat the chocolate in the microwave for one minute at 30 percent power, stir it, then check the temperature with an instant-read thermometer. Next, heat it in ten- to twenty-second intervals, testing the temperature until just right. Cullen warms Valrhona to 131°, but most brands should be heated no higher than 120° for dark chocolate, 110° for milk or white. Every brand has its own specifications; call the manufacturer for details. You can also melt chocolate in a bowl set over—not in—simmering water. Never cover chocolate; if steam collects, it will ruin it.

2. Pour two-thirds of the melted chocolate onto a marble slab. (You can also use a Corian, Formica, or stainless-steel surface.) Spread it into a thin layer with an offset spatula. The goal is to lower the temperature to 80° to 83°, depending on the type of chocolate. The cocoa butter will begin to "seed," or solidify in a stable form. Use an instant-read thermometer to check the temperature.

3. Scrape the cooled chocolate back into bowl with remaining chocolate; blend thoroughly. Aim for a temperature of 86° to 91°. At that point, the chocolate is tempered and should be used immediately. Temperature must be maintained throughout the molding process; rest the bowl on a heating pad with extra cushioning to protect it from overheating. Keep the thermometer in the chocolate to monitor the temperature while you work.

ABOVE: **A batch of chocolate shells being made in their molds; they are filled with dark-chocolate ganache.** OPPOSITE: **The basic technique for tempering; for the very best results, use only the finest quality chocolate.**

WORKING WITH MOLDS

Since chocolate reflects the texture and shape of any surface, clean, smooth molds are important. Use a soft cotton cloth to wipe them out, and cotton swabs for crevices.

After a mold is filled with chocolate, let it set until hardened. To remove the chocolates from the mold, invert it gently onto a plate. Chocolate shrinks as it sets, so the chocolates should come right out. Until you remove the chocolate from the mold, you can't be certain that you tempered it perfectly. Fortunately, only beauty and texture are affected, so even mistakes are delicious.

MAKING FILLED CHOCOLATES

Chocolate shells can be filled with berries, nuts, or white- or dark-chocolate ganache. **(1)** To make shells for filled chocolates, pipe tempered chocolate (see opposite page for tempering instructions) into a mold. Drop the filled mold gently on the work surface to force out bubbles. **(2)** Let stand for two minutes, then turn the mold upside down and shake out excess chocolate, using a circular motion to make sure the mold is coated evenly. **(3)** Scrape across the top of the mold with an offset spatula, then place the mold face down, so the chocolate shells thicken at their bases, on a level baking sheet covered with parchment paper. Refrigerate for ten to twenty minutes, allowing chocolate to set. **(4)** Fill the shells almost to the top with room-temperature ganache (recipes on page 87), or add a whole nut or berry. If using ganache, drop the mold gently on the work surface to level the ganache. **(5)** Pipe in more tempered chocolate, filling the mold and sealing the chocolates. Scrape the top with an offset spatula, removing the excess tempered chocolate and leveling the bottoms of molded chocolates. Refrigerate ten to twenty minutes before unmolding.

MAKING SHAPED CHOCOLATES

Each component of the confections shown on these pages must be made with tempered chocolate (see instructions on page 90). Store finished chocolates in an airtight container in a cool, dry place (but not in the refrigerator), and use any leftover chocolate for other baking needs.

VINE LETTERS To make dark-chocolate letters decorated with white-chocolate vines *(opposite, top left)*, pipe garlands of white chocolate into a letter mold, beginning each segment at the leaf and then trailing to the stem **(1)**. Refrigerate for five minutes; fill molds with tempered dark chocolate.

TULIPS White-chocolate tulips *(opposite, top right)* can be filled with ice cream, mousse, or any soft dessert. Blow up balloons, twist ends, and clamp with binder clips. This will allow you to let the air out slowly; if the balloon pops, the chocolate tulip will shatter. Line a baking sheet with parchment paper. Using a pastry bag, drop a dot of white chocolate (86°) the size of a quarter on the sheet. Holding a balloon at a forty-five-degree angle, drag it through the bowl of chocolate to make a petal **(2)**. Lift out balloon, rotate it, and drag it through again to make another petal. Make three to five petals, then set the balloon on the dot. Repeat process. When the tray is full, refrigerate for twenty minutes. Unclip the balloons, and let the air out gently, peeling balloon from the chocolate if necessary; dab chocolate at base if the balloon leaves a hole.

NEST AND EGGS This chocolate-nest center-piece *(opposite, bottom left)* can hold a chocolate egg for each dinner guest. The nest is built on a dark-chocolate shell formed on a round balloon. Blow up, and clip a balloon with a binder clip. This will allow you to let the air out slowly; if the balloon pops, the chocolate nest will shatter. Dunk the end of the balloon straight down in dark chocolate, wait a minute, and dunk it again. Turn balloon, clip-side down, and

rest it on a small bowl; refrigerate to set. To make twigs, begin by covering cookie sheets with parchment paper (you will need a total of five sheets of twigs). Dip your fingers into dark chocolate, and wave your hand over the lined cookie sheet, trailing chocolate over the entire surface. Refrigerate for five to ten minutes. Unclip the balloon, and gently let the air out; peel the balloon from the chocolate shell if it doesn't come away on its own. Remove the twigs from the parchment **(3)**. Build the nest by slinging some tempered chocolate on the base, then add twigs in layers. The eggs are white chocolate poured into molds that have been sponged with milk chocolate (see acorn directions below). The two halves of the eggs are made separately, then joined with a dab of white chocolate.

ACORNS AND LEAVES Mottled acorns and leaves *(opposite, bottom right)* are made by first dabbing milk chocolate into the molds, using a small natural sponge or clean small paintbrush **(4)**. Refrigerate five minutes; then pipe tempered dark chocolate into molds.

CHOCOLATE CUPS Cups of dark chocolate (shown on page 87) are filled with white-chocolate ganache and are topped with a dusting of cocoa. To make cups, follow directions for filled chocolates on page 91, but instead of inverting the shells when you refrigerate them, leave them right-side up. After twenty minutes (or when set), lift each cup out, pipe in room-temperature white ganache, and sprinkle with cocoa.

GAME PIECES First form the dots or suits of game pieces (shown on page 89) by filling a pastry bag and piping white or dark chocolate into the appropriate indentations in the molds. Chill for ten minutes; then pipe in the other kind of chocolate.

GIFTS & WRAPPING

W
rapping gifts is a holiday ritual to be savored. With each crease of paper and each
bow you tie, you are creating a delicious mystery, making a gift at once
anonymous and personal, untouchable and inviting. As they multiply beneath
the tree, gifts embody the excitement and suspense that we wait for all year.

A wrapped gift gives no clues to its contents, nor should it. Every present, however humble
or extravagant, deserves to be wrapped with care and creativity. First, make sure you have all
the supplies you need, such as scissors, pinking shears, tape, and an array of papers and ribbons.
You'll be better prepared if you collect and save ribbons throughout the year (just iron used
ribbons to make them look brand-new) and if you buy wrapping paper when you see a sheet or
roll you love, not just when you need some. But keep in mind that fancier doesn't necessarily
mean better: Inexpensive sheets of tissue, glassine, kraft paper, and waxed paper add simple
beauty to any package; waxed twine, seam binding, and rickrack make simple, pretty bows.

Some of the best packages are those that can be used again, like the felt wrappings shown in
this chapter. They make lovely presents on their own, but if you can't resist nestling a little
trinket in one of these soft boxes and bags, a single present becomes two. Stockings may be the
cleverest wrapping of all. What could be better than something made expressly to be filled with
gifts? Use the ideas and instructions here to make stockings for your family, your friends,
yourself. They'll soon be as beloved a part of Christmas as the oldest ornament on the tree.

The gift enclosed in any wrapping should be special, too—and if you make it yourself, it will be.
When you tuck it under the tree, your work is done, but for someone else, the anticipation begins.

ABOVE: **A dramatic tower of wrapped boxes is bound with two beautiful ribbons; each box is wrapped
first in colored tissue paper, then frosted over with a sheet of glassine, available by the sheet or roll.** PREVIOUS
PAGES, LEFT AND RIGHT: **Several small gifts dangle enticingly from a length of ribbon. A stack of scented pillows.**

PRESENTS ON A STRING Presented this way (see page 94), small gifts labeled with numbers or names add to the excitement of the holidays. Start by wrapping the gifts and tying each one with a ribbon bow. Use rubber stamps or a pen to label small tags with consecutive numbers—for the twelve days of Christmas or the eight days of Hanukkah, for example—or names. Tie or glue the tags onto the gifts. Then tie a length of thin ribbon, waxed twine, or pretty cord to all of the gifts, connecting them; leave extra at the top to hang from a doorknob or mantel.

SCENTED BALSAM PILLOWS Pillows stuffed with balsam, cedar tips, or lavender **(1)** fill a home with a fresh scent all year long. Use luxurious fabrics, such as soft wool or beautiful silk, for these gifts. Large ones make good throw pillows; use small ones as sachets. **(2)** Cut two pieces of material to the same size, just larger than you want the pillow to be; we used different colors for the front and back. A 12-inch square is good for a throw pillow; use smaller squares and rectangles for sachets. Pin together the two pieces with the right sides facing. Sew around the perimeter with a ½-inch seam allowance, leaving a 2-inch opening on one side. Clip the corners and trim the seam allowance, if necessary, to make the fabric lie flat. Turn pillowcase right-side out. **(3)** Roll stiff paper into a cone shape, tape it together, and use it as a funnel to fill the pillow with balsam, cedar tips, lavender, or any combination. Stitch the opening closed by hand.

RICE-PAPER ENVELOPE This slender package *(below)* is made from a sheet of heavy, textured paper folded around a tissue-wrapped gift. The outer layer is a 12-by-27-inch piece of Japanese kozo paper (commonly known as rice paper) backed with green paper. Use a ruler or bone folder, available at art-supply stores, to make neat creases 9, 12, and 21 inches from a short side of the paper. Enclose gift, bind package with a wide satin ribbon, and finish with a slim ribbon tied in a knot.

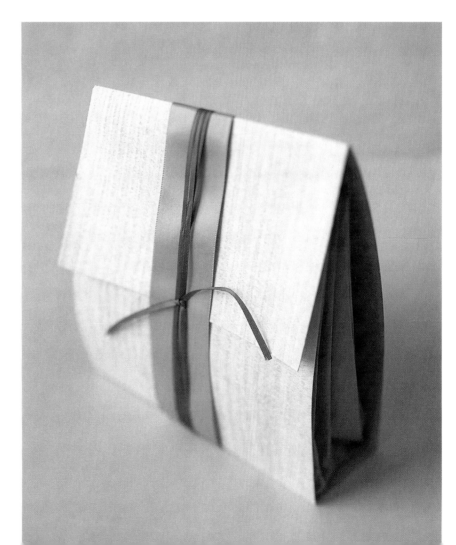

TULLE WRAPPING A square of tulle makes a fabulous package out of a plain one *(right)*. The sheer net fabric is available in many colors; better yet, it is very inexpensive. First wrap a box in plain paper or tissue paper. Place the box in the center of a square of tulle (or two squares of tulle for a fuller top), gather excess fabric on top of box, and cinch with a rubber band. Hide the rubber band with a ribbon, and tie a Christmas ball or other ornament into the bow.

TINSEL STARS Give gifts a little sparkle with tinsel *(below)*. Twist wired tinsel (available at specialty craft stores) into stars. For one with six points, cut three pieces of tinsel, two of equal length and one a little longer. Twist equal pieces together at centers, and wrap third one onto the two, forming a star. Bend the end of the longer piece into a hook, and attach the star from the ribbon on a gift. These stars can also be hung on the tree.

METALLIC TRIMMINGS Gifts wrapped in cool, icy hues bring a wintry elegance to the collection beneath the tree *(opposite)*. Tie tinsel around a box instead of ribbon, and add an initialed aluminum tag. Slip a stick of candy into a bow of shimmering striped ribbon. Tuck the stem of leaf into a neat knot. To make aluminum tag and leaf, see the directions on page 42.

"ENGRAVED" GIFT TAGS So much effort goes into choosing Christmas gifts—and then on go those store-bought gift tags, which always look like an afterthought. Here's a much nicer alternative using a product available at most craft stores: embossing powder. The basic technique involves a dusting of the silver powder and a little heat; the result is a raised design in a deep shade of silver *(right)*. This method can also be used for making placecards and note-cards. You'll need a rubber stamp in the shape of a border or other decoration, and an ink pad; we used one with clear ink, but tinted ink would also work. **(1)** Stamp the design on a piece of heavy paper. **(2)** Sprinkle embossing powder generously over the design. **(3)** Tilt the dusted paper to remove the excess powder, which can be used again. Use a fine paintbrush to remove any stray powder. **(4)** Using tongs, hold paper 4 to 6 inches above a hot plate or electric burner on medium heat. As the powder melts, it will turn from a dull, dark silver to a lighter, three-dimensional metallic surface; this takes about 3 to 4 minutes. Cut out the tag, and add a ribbon—and a name.

gingerbread GIFT TAGS

makes 30 to 40

- *1   cup (2 sticks) unsalted butter*
- *1   cup dark-brown sugar, packed*
- *4   teaspoons ground ginger*
- *4   teaspoons ground cinnamon*
- *1½ teaspoons ground cloves*
- *1   teaspoon finely ground black pepper*
- *1½ teaspoons salt*
- *2   large eggs*
- *¾   cup plus 2 tablespoons unsulfured molasses*
- *6   cups all-purpose flour*

1. In the bowl of an electric mixer, use the paddle attachment to cream butter and sugar until mixture is fluffy. Mix in ginger, cinnamon, cloves, pepper, and salt. Beat in the eggs and molasses.

2. Add flour; mix on low speed to combine. Divide dough into thirds, press to flatten, and wrap in plastic. Transfer to refrigerator, and chill for at least 1 hour.

3. Heat oven to 350°. Flour two pieces of parchment. Roll out each piece of dough to ⅛ inch on floured parchment. Cover with another sheet of parchment, and place in freezer for 15 minutes.

4. Remove from freezer, and use cookie cutters to cut into desired shapes. Using a spatula, transfer shapes to a parchment-lined baking sheet. (Do not move shapes again; if the dough becomes too soft to work with, return to freezer until firm.) If desired, use alphabet cookie cutters to cut initials from the centers of the cookies. Make an ⅛-inch hole for the ribbon (a #7 round pastry tip works well). Cover cookies with parchment; place a second baking pan on top of parchment to keep cookies flat while baking.

5. Bake until lightly browned, about 35 minutes for a single batch in center of oven, or 40 to 45 minutes with two batches in oven, rotating them twice between shelves. Transfer to a wire rack; do not remove top pan until cookies are cool, about 20 minutes.

ABOVE: These edible gift tags are sure to be appreciated. LEFT: Use large alphabet cookie cutters to make letter-shape gingerbread tags, or smaller ones for letter cutouts in a tree or wreath shape. Don't forget to make a hole in dough before baking so you can pull a string through the cookie and tie it into the bow.

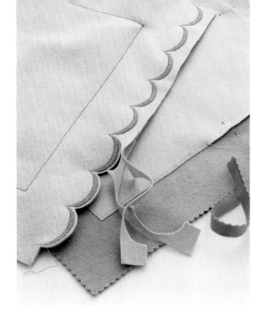

WORKING WITH FELT

Dense, thick felt never unravels and doesn't need to be hemmed, making it versatile and easy to work with. Most felt is blended with inexpensive materials, such as rayon or polyester, but pure wool felt, which was used for all of the projects on these pages, is a fabric worth seeking out. It will produce the most beautiful, long-lasting results. We recommend using a size-14 needle and 100 percent polyester thread on the sewing machine. For many of these projects, scalloped shears were used for a decorative edge, but pinking shears can be used instead.

FELT PILLOWS Measure your pillow and add 1 inch (or more, for a bigger flange) to each side. Cut two felt squares to that dimension; sew together along three sides using a zigzag stitch. Insert the pillow, and sew up the fourth side. Finish edges *(opposite)* with sewing-machine stitches, blanket-stitch with yarn, or trim with pinking shears; see page 133 for a scallop-edge template. If you wish to finish pillows with a ball fringe, stitch it in when sewing up sides. For a removable cover, cut a long slit in the middle of back panel, and zigzag the edges of the slit before sewing front and back together; insert the pillow through the slit. To finish the scalloped edge and the contrasting edge *(above)*: Trim excess fabric from scalloping created by a sewing machine. Center and sew the front panel, which is the pillow's size, onto larger back panel.

FELT BOOK WRAPS Make felt jackets *(above)* for all the books you give for Christmas this year, including journals, photo albums, and guest books. The size of the felt depends entirely on the size of the book: Cut a rectangle of felt tall enough to cover the book, extending an additional ¼ inch beyond the top and bottom, and long enough to wrap around the book and fold inside both the front and back covers. Fold the sides in, and pin *(right)*. Zigzag around the perimeter of jacket. Add a felt strap with a button or loop of ribbon to secure. The tassel, which is laced through an eyelet on the bookmark, is made from a 6-by-2-inch length of felt with a 1-inch-deep fringe cut along one side, then rolled tightly around a cord and secured with a few stitches. The other end of the cord is then knotted through an eyelet.

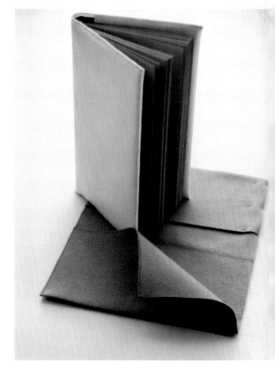

FELT BOXES These soft boxes *(above left)* pay homage to the Shaker design philosophy: Simple shapes executed in good-quality materials are the most beautiful objects. Cut out a circle of felt for the bottom of the box *(left)*. Multiply diameter (ours is 5½ inches across) by 3.14 to find the circumference. For sides, cut out a felt rectangle: The length should be the circumference plus double the width of your zigzag stitch for the seam allowance; the width is the desired height. Sew short ends of rectangle together using a zigzag stitch. Pin one edge to felt circle; sew with a zigzag stitch. Trim the top with pinking shears. To make lid, repeat the steps above, starting with circle that is just a bit bigger so it will fit over the bottom half.

FELT BOTTLE BAGS Wrapping a bottle of wine or champagne is always a problem. At last—here's a beautiful solution. To make these bags *(above right)*, follow instructions on this page for the felt boxes, making the bottom of the bag a bit bigger than the bottom of the bottle and the sides about 2 inches higher than the bottle is tall. To finish the tops, cinch closed with ribbon or cord, or cut slits and weave the ribbon through. On the dark-green bag, thin roping is laced through large eyelets, and felt leaves are sewn to the end of the cord (see page 133 for the leaf template); stitch "veins" along the leaves as shown. The matte surface of wool-felt bottle bags contrasts beautifully with glossy velvet and satin ribbons.

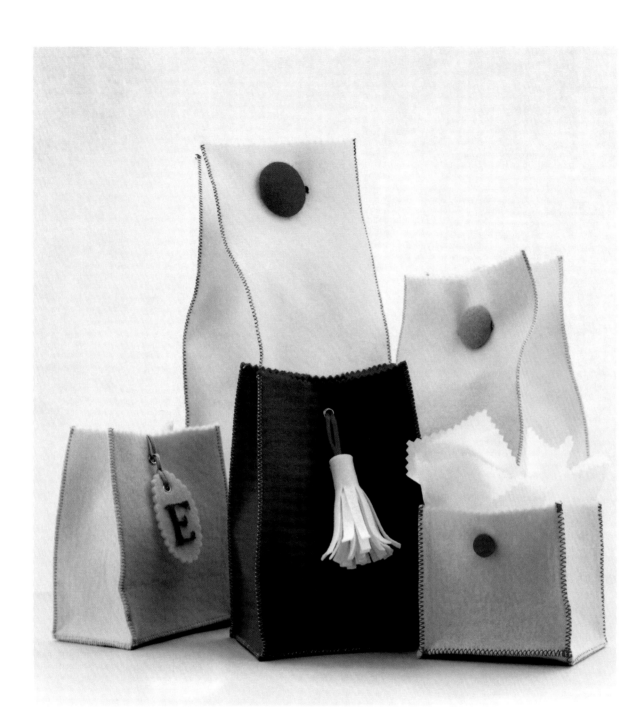

FELT BAGS These sacks *(above)* are modeled after the classic brown paper bag. Each one is made from three pieces of felt: One piece is for the front, bottom, and back; the other two are the sides. For a bag that's 8 inches tall, 5 inches wide, and 3½ inches deep, the piece for the front, bottom, and back should be 19½ inches long and 5 inches wide; side pieces are 8 by 3½ inches. Fold the large piece where the corners will be. Use zigzag stitch to "pinch" the folds *(right)*, using contrasting thread, if desired. Pin sides in place, then zigzag in place. Trim bag tops with pinking shears. Leave bags open at the top, or add a closure. Put a buttonhole in front of bag; cover a button with felt or other fabric, and sew it on. Or add eyelets, lace cord through, and finish with a tassel or felt medallion. To make a tassel, refer to the instructions for felt book wraps on page 103. When working with felt, dust the work area first, since felt is a magnet for lint.

Refer to templates and general instructions on pages 133 and 134; follow directions below.

CHILD'S STOCKING This stocking *(right)* is 1 foot long, just large enough for a few precious gifts; it was made using the boot template. Cut out front and back of the stocking and cuff pieces, adding ½-inch seam allowance to stocking pieces and ¼-inch seam allowance to the cuff pieces. Cut a piece of felt using scalloped template. To cover buttons with velvet, you'll need a covered-button kit *(below right)*, available from sewing stores. Sew buttons onto front piece of stocking. Sew front and back together; trim seam allowance with scalloped or pinking shears. Sew cuff to stocking. Sew pearl buttons to scalloped edge; use fabric glue or fusible interfacing to attach to cuff, hiding ends in back. For tassel, refer to instructions for felt book wraps on page 103.

MONOGRAM STOCKING This personalized stocking *(opposite, left)* is 20 inches long, made from the sock template. Cut front and back of stocking in different colors; the front piece doesn't need a seam allowance; cut the back piece 1 inch wider all around. Cut a monogram from felt, and glue it to front of stocking. To make mock cuff, use scalloped or pinking shears to cut a piece of felt as wide as front of stocking; cut a piece of ribbon ½ inch longer. Center ribbon on cuff piece, fold ends of ribbon under ends of felt, and iron flat. Pin cuff to front of stocking, pin front to back, and zigzag around perimeter of front piece. Cut out decorative edge of back piece with scalloped or pinking shears.

POLKA-DOT STOCKING Use any colors you like for the stocking base and dots *(opposite, center)*. Cover buttons in felt. Cut front and back pieces of stocking, adding a ½-inch seam allowance; cut cuff pieces, adding a ¼-inch seam allowance. Sew buttons to front piece. Topstitch front and back together; trim seam allowance with scalloped or pinking shears. To make cuff, topstitch velvet

ribbon to cuff pieces, and trim bottom edge of cuff pieces with scalloped or pinking shears. Sew cuff to stocking.

DAISY STOCKING This cheerful stocking *(opposite, right)* can be dotted with a few daisies, or covered with them. Cover buttons with velvet; cut out daisies. Cut out front and back of stocking and cuff pieces (add ¼-inch seam allowance to cuff pieces only). Poke metal loop of buttons through center of daisies; then sew onto front of stocking. Zigzag front to back along edge. Sew cuff to stocking. Cut a piece of felt using scalloped template, and attach to cuff with glue or fusible interfacing, hiding ends in back.

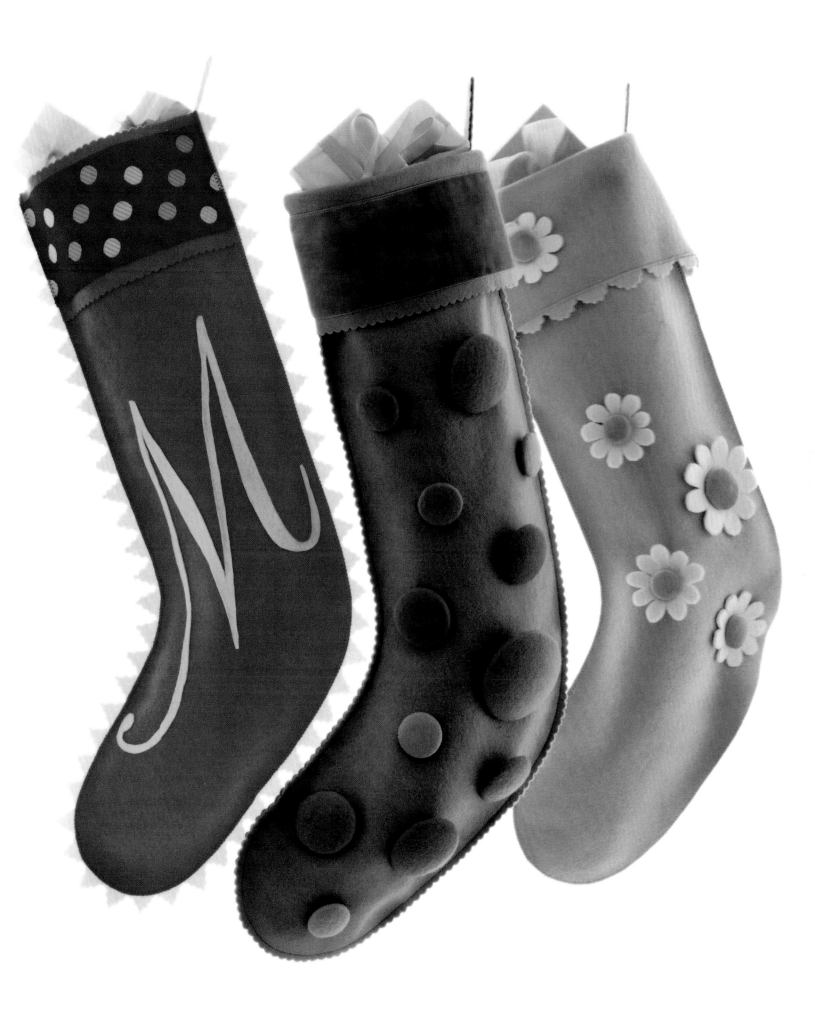

TEA-TOWEL STOCKINGS Linen tea towels make homey stockings *(opposite)*. **(1)** Use traditional stocking template on page 134 to cut out front and back of stocking, adding ½-inch seam allowance, from a new or vintage tea towel. For the cuff, cut two pieces that are double the width of stocking's top, plus 1 inch. If using a fringed towel edge for cuff, cut just one piece. **(2)** Pin stocking pieces with right sides facing, and sew along sides. Pin cuff pieces with right sides facing, sew three sides, leaving one long edge open, and turn right-side out. **(3)** Wrap cuff around top of inside-out stocking. Pin and sew cuff to stocking along top edge; sew vertical edges of cuff. Turn stocking right-side out, fold the cuff over, and iron flat.

EMBROIDERED SNOWFLAKE STOCKING This stocking *(right)* starts with a plain wool sock. Fit the sock with a 4-inch embroidery hoop. Beginning on inside, make three intersecting 3-inch stitches, creating six "branches." Secure stitches with a small horizontal stitch at intersection. Make two ½-inch diagonal stitches on each side of the six branches. Tie a French knot at the end of each branch: Bring needle from inside sock to outside. Hold yarn with one hand and needle with the other. Place needle beneath the yarn that extends between your hand and sock; hold needle against the yarn, perpendicular to it. Angle needle toward sock, and move needle so yarn nearest sock wraps around it two to five times (the number of wraps determines the knot's size). The loose end of the yarn will be closer to top of needle; bring yarn under the needle, and wrap back over the needle near its point. Insert needle through the sock close to where it came out; pull yarn all the way through, being careful not to pull knot through sock. Tie off on back. To make a twisted loop: Fold a 3-foot length of yarn in half. Hold ends together in one hand, and twist looped end about 30 to 40 times. Let the twisted yarn fold in half **(1)**, creating a double-twisted strand. Knot looped end and loose ends together **(2)**. Fold in half again, then stitch inside stocking.

PACKING AND SHIPPING TIPS

With some presents, gift wrapping is only the beginning. Any present that will be mailed must be wrapped again, this time in a sturdy outer shipping box. This second layer isn't about beauty—it's pure protection. Many of the delicate gifts sent at this time of year are foods, such as cookies and jars of jam, which require some special treatment. The ideas given below for packing them can also be applied to other breakables.

PACKING MATERIALS Give every gift two lines of defense: It should be well packed in an inner gift box, then packed in a second, outer shipping box that will see it safely through the mail. The golden rule of packing is to choose a box appropriate in size to the item it will contain. Whenever you give something the chance to shift, you also give it the chance to break.

Allow about two to three inches between the inner and outer boxes, on all sides. The space should be filled with a packing material that will cushion the box's contents. There are several choices for padding. Traditional foam peanuts are still commonly used and very effective, though not environmentally friendly. A product called Eco-Foam can be used instead; however, these biodegradable packing peanuts melt if they get wet, so

they shouldn't be used for anything that could leak. Other good choices include excelsior, a shredded wood-fiber product, and wood shavings, which are better with light objects since heavy ones could crush them. Kraft paper or newspaper can be crumpled into balls and used as padding. Popcorn is another good alternative for smaller boxes; for packing, always air-pop the corn without oil, which could attract pests. Bubble Wrap is excellent for wrapping breakables and lining boxes. With the exception of popcorn, packing materials—and boxes, too—should be recycled; save what you receive to use the next time you send a gift.

SHIPPING BOXES After you pack the gift into the shipping box with packing materials, seal box along seams with two-inch-wide pressure-sensitive tape. Tape the bottom seams as well as the top. Don't tie the box with rope or string, which can get snagged on sorting machines. Affix the mailing label on the surface of the box itself, not on a seam or sealing tape. If you're reusing a box, be sure to cross off the old mailing and return addresses. It's a good idea to tuck another mailing label inside the box before sealing it; this will help the gift find its destination even if it gets damaged and the outside label is lost.

ABOVE, LEFT TO RIGHT: Two to three inches of packing material, such as Bubble Wrap, protect a gift and keep it from shifting. A steamed Christmas pudding can be sent in the mold it was made in; cover the top of the pudding with parchment or waxed paper secured tightly with string or ribbon before placing the lid on the mold to prevent seepage, and pack the mold into a box cushioned with excelsior. Wrap the gift boxes in an additional layer of tissue for extra protection against nicks and rips.

COOKIES When packing cookies, choose a box that will hold them snugly. Cut a panel of small Bubble Wrap to the shape of box, and fit it into the bottom. In alternating directions, line the box with lengths of waxed paper or parchment that come up the sides and out; you will fold them over the contents before you close the box. Place a layer of cookies into the box, edge to edge; don't crowd or stack them. Cover with a piece of waxed paper or parchment cut to the shape of the box. Repeat the layers to within an inch of the top of the box. Cover the last layer of cookies with paper and Bubble Wrap, fold the paper flaps over the top of the contents, and place the top on the box.

JARS AND BOTTLES For gifts in bottles or jars, such as flavored oils or preserves, leakage can be a problem. Martha places jars of preserves in individual resealable plastic bags. Each bagged jar is then wrapped in small Bubble Wrap. Jars are nestled into a sturdy box filled with cushioning, such as an inexpensive wooden box filled with excelsior. There should be sufficient padding between the jars as well as between the jars and the sides of the box. Always cushion contents both on the bottom and the top of a box. Professionals sometimes use a protective

cushion called a French roll for breakable items. To make a French roll, begin by lightly crumpling several pieces of tissue paper, then roll them inside a single sheet of tissue, forming a long, soft pad. Make enough French rolls so that, when laid side to side, they make a surface that is wider than the object is long. Lay the object down at the end of the rolls, and roll the object up in them. When you reach the end, wrap the entire bundle in two more sheets of tissue paper, and secure with a piece of tape. Another double layer of Bubble Wrap provides even more protection.

SHIPPING RESTRICTIONS Be aware that some shipping services, including the U.S. Postal Service, have restrictions on the size and weight of packages. Most major services maintain toll-free numbers for questions. Because of increased security precautions, the U.S. Postal Service now requires that, for all parcels greater than sixteen ounces, you send them directly from a post office branch rather than leave them in a mailbox. Millions of packages are sent every December; to make sure that yours arrives on time, plan ahead. Mailing your gifts just after Thanksgiving isn't too early, and it will put your mind at ease. At the latest, have them in the mail by the second week of December.

BELOW, LEFT TO RIGHT: To prevent cookies from crumbling, layer pieces of parchment between them, and line the box with Bubble Wrap. A single fragile cookie should be wrapped first in parchment or waxed paper, then in Bubble Wrap; nestle it into a shallow box filled with thin wood shavings or other padding. To protect against spills and breaking, jam jars are individually bagged and then wrapped in Bubble Wrap before being packed in a sturdy, cushioned box.

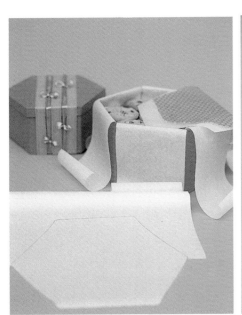

NEW YEAR'S DAY AT HOME

J ust a week has passed since Christmas. You're refreshed, relaxed, and wholly satisfied from all the feasts, sweets, and leftovers of the season. The hustle and bustle have been replaced by a content calm. It's the perfect time to throw another party: a casual, come-on-over kind of party, an open house. What better way to close the holiday season and start the new year than surrounded by friends and family amid the comforts of home?

The decorations are still up; the tree is still sparkling. All you have to do is supply the food, and even that isn't so hard. After hosting more than twenty New Year's Day get-togethers, Joy and Robert Lewis, friends and neighbors of Martha's, have it down to a science. "We call it an 'At Home,' which is very English, because we like the idea of being at home with our neighbors, having a relaxed and easy time," says Joy. To prepare, Joy spends a day gathering foods such as cheeses, nuts, dried fruits, and meats from her favorite purveyors.

Joy has her own sources, and you may have yours. If not, just look around. All across the country there are specialty-food stores, butchers, bakeries, and wonderful mail-order catalogs that are there to do the work for you. Prepare a roast turkey or glazed ham as the main course (see pages 126 to 131) and serve it with thick slices of country bread and an array of mustards and chutneys. Serve hearty salads made with wild rice, bulghur, or couscous. Splurge on smoked salmon and caviar. For dessert, follow Joy and Robert's lead: Let friends bring their specialties.

Make sure you have enough food to replenish the buffet as often as it needs it. Guests will come and go, eat and drink, and relax and chat throughout the afternoon. Settled into the sofa or curled up by the fire, they are certain to have one more plate of cake and cookies and another glass of apple cider as the new year gets off to a gentle, sweet start.

ABOVE: Reminiscent of a slower time, a silver tray collects guests' calling cards. PREVIOUS PAGES, LEFT AND RIGHT: A cozy corner in the library is scented with fragrant narcissi. In a festive centerpiece, citrus fruits are arranged on stacked cake plates; the draped ribbons of orange rind are made by carving an orange in a spiral with a citrus stripper.

ABOVE, CLOCKWISE FROM TOP LEFT: The Lewises' Greek Revival home in Sag Harbor, New York. Old family photos perch on the mantel. Two Dresdens, German ornaments made of embossed cardboard, are more than one hundred years old. Each guest receives a vintage New Year's card. Antique ornaments in Paris compotes.

ABOVE: A casual gathering like an open house doesn't require an elaborate bar. Hosts Joy and Robert Lewis set out bottles of Riesling wine on a butler's tray and also offer their guests fresh apple cider and eggnog. Holiday touches appear throughout the house, such as the holly sprigs tucked behind this English botanical painting. OPPOSITE: A white goose-feather tree, made in Germany in the 1890s, is trimmed with the Lewises' colorful collection of antique ornaments.

APPLE *and* RED-ONION
caraway TART

makes 2 tarts; serves 16 to 20

2½ cups all-purpose flour

2 teaspoons salt

1½ teaspoons whole caraway seeds

1 cup (2 sticks) cold unsalted butter,
cut into small pieces, plus 4 tablespoons
for filling
Ice water (¼ to ½ cup)

4 Granny Smith apples

4 medium red onions (about 6 ounces
each)

1 tablespoon plus 1 teaspoon sugar

½ teaspoon freshly ground pepper

2 ounces blue cheese, crumbled
Vegetable-oil cooking spray

1. Place flour, 1 teaspoon salt, and 1 teaspoon caraway seeds in a food processor. Add butter pieces; process for about 10 seconds, until mixture resembles coarse meal.

2. With machine running, add ice water slowly through feed tube. When dough holds together but is not sticky, stop adding water; do not process for more than 30 seconds.

3. Divide dough in half; turn out onto plastic wrap. Press dough into flat rectangles. Wrap in plastic, and chill for at least an hour.

4. Spray two rectangular tart pans (13¼ by 3¾ inches) with vegetable-oil cooking spray; place on a parchment-lined baking sheet. On a floured board, roll pastry to a thickness of ⅛ inch. Transfer a piece of pastry to each pan, pressing it into edges; trim pastry about ⅜ inch higher than edge of pan. Prick bottom of tart. Chill for at least 30 minutes or up to 24 hours (covered with plastic).

5. Heat oven to 400°; place rack in center. Line chilled pastry with foil, and weight with dried beans. Bake for about 20 minutes; when pastry just colors around edges, remove foil and weights; continue to bake just until pastry is light golden, about 10 more minutes. Cool completely on a wire rack.

6. To make the filling, peel and core apples. Cut into quarters; then cut each quarter into four slices. Peel onions, and halve lengthwise. Cut each half into ¼-inch slices. Melt sugar and 2 tablespoons butter in a medium skillet. Add apples; cook over medium-low heat for 8 minutes, stirring occasionally. Add ½ teaspoon salt and ¼ teaspoon pepper; raise heat to medium high, and cook for 2 more minutes, until the apples are golden. Transfer apples and all the pan juices to a bowl. In the same skillet, melt remaining 2 tablespoons butter. Add onions and cook for 8 minutes, stirring occasionally, until onions are just brown. Add remaining ½ teaspoon salt and ¼ teaspoon pepper; cook 2 minutes more. Return apples to pan; over low heat, toss to combine.

7. Sprinkle cheese along bottom of tart shells. Divide warm apple-onion mixture between them. Sprinkle remaining ½ teaspoon caraway seeds over tarts, and serve.

triple-crème CHEESE
with armagnac-soaked RAISINS

serves 8 to 10

The raisins can be soaked for up to a
month before serving.

½ cup golden raisins

¼ cup Armagnac, a French brandy

1 whole rindless triple-crème cheese
(1½ pounds), such as Brillat-Savarin

1. In a glass container, combine raisins and Armagnac. Cover, and let stand for 24 hours; refrigerate if not using immediately.

2. Let cheese come to room temperature. Just before serving, pour raisins and Armagnac over cheese. Serve with crackers.

WILD-RICE SALAD

serves 8 to 10

A good addition to a buffet, this salad has a
flavor that develops as it stands at
room temperature.

 3   *cups wild rice*
 1½ *teaspoons salt, plus extra for*
      boiling water
 4   *blood or navel oranges*
 3   *tablespoons red-wine vinegar*
 3   *tablespoons sherry vinegar*
 1   *teaspoon freshly ground pepper*
 ½   *cup extra-virgin olive oil*
 6   *scallions, cut into ⅛-inch rounds*
 1   *cup dried cranberries*
 1   *bunch flat-leaf parsley, leaves finely*
      chopped (½ cup)

1. Cook the wild rice in a large pot of salted
boiling water until just tender, about 40
minutes. Drain in a colander.
2. Meanwhile, cut away peel and pith from
oranges; holding oranges over a bowl to
catch the juice, remove segments from white
membrane; place segments in the bowl.
3. Combine vinegars, 1½ teaspoons salt, and
pepper in a bowl. Slowly whisk in olive oil.
4. In a large serving bowl, combine wild rice,
scallions, dried cranberries, parsley, and
orange sections as well as their juice. Drizzle
vinaigrette over mixture; gently toss; serve.

TOP: Segments of blood oranges add brilliant color and sweetness to the wild-rice salad. ABOVE, LEFT:
Hosts Joy and Robert Lewis—she is president of a stationery company called Mrs. John L. Strong of
New York; he is an interior designer—believe their annual "at-home" gathering is as close to effort-
less as holiday entertaining can be. ABOVE, RIGHT: Martha helps a young guest choose dessert.
OPPOSITE, TOP TO BOTTOM: Savory tarts, like this one made with apples and red onions, make great
party food, as they are delicious served at room temperature. A rich triple-crème cheese is topped
with golden raisins that have been soaked in Armagnac, a French brandy. A trip to the buffet yields
a full plate, which includes slices of ham and turkey, wild-rice salad, and a wedge of cheese.

almond CRESCENTS

makes about 40 cookies

2¼   cups all-purpose flour

⅛   teaspoon salt

½   cup (3 ounces) blanched almonds

⅔   cup superfine sugar

14   tablespoons (1¾ sticks) cold unsalted
     butter, cut into very small pieces

3   large egg yolks

1   teaspoon pure vanilla extract

¼   cup confectioners' sugar for sifting

1. Sift flour and salt. In a food processor, grind almonds fine. Add sugar and sifted flour and salt. Pulse to combine. With machine running, slowly add pieces of butter through feed tube. Add yolks and vanilla; process for 20 seconds. Divide dough into two pieces. Roll each into a 1½-inch-thick log, wrap in plastic, and refrigerate for 3 hours.
2. Line two baking sheets with parchment paper. Cut dough into ⅜-inch-thick pieces. Pinch each piece into 3-inch crescent; place on baking sheets, 1 inch apart. Refrigerate for 30 minutes.
3. Heat oven to 350°. Bake crescents for 10 minutes, then rotate sheets between oven shelves, and bake about 8 minutes more; cookies should not brown. Transfer parchment with cookies to a wire rack; let cool 5 minutes. Sift confectioners' sugar over cookies before serving.

ABOVE: **This plate of sweets includes (clockwise from top) almond torte, almond crescents, chocolate-studded rehrücken, and hartshorn cookies.** RIGHT: **These pure-white cookies are springerle, first made in Bavaria, Austria, and Switzerland almost four hundred years ago; their raised design is created by pressing a mold into the dough (see recipe on page 77).** OPPOSITE: **Presented simply but beautifully, this buffet is easy for the hosts to replenish; the citrus centerpiece provides a cheerful focal point.**

ABOVE: **A selection of dried and glacéed fruits, such as kumquats, citrus slices, and citron melon, makes a tempting, colorful addition to the buffet; their shiny surfaces and the glass cake stands reflect the clear winter light streaming through a nearby window.**

chocolate-studded REHRUCKEN

makes 3 loaves

Rehrücken means "saddle of venison"; it refers to the shape of the loaf pan used to make these traditional Austrian cakes.

- ½   *cup sliced blanched almonds, toasted*
- 1¾ *cups plus 4 tablespoons (3½ sticks) unsalted butter*
- 14 *ounces almond paste*
- ¼   *cup plus 1 tablespoon confectioners' sugar*
- 1½ *teaspoons salt*
- 1½ *teaspoons pure vanilla extract*
      Zest of 2 lemons
- 10 *large eggs, separated*
- 3   *tablespoons orange-flavored liqueur, such as Grand Marnier or Cointreau*
- ⅓   *cup cornstarch*
- 3   *cups plus 3 tablespoons all-purpose flour*
- 1⅓ *cups granulated sugar*
- 11½ *ounces bittersweet chocolate, coarsely chopped (2 cups)*
- ⅓   *cup finely chopped crystallized ginger*
      Vegetable-oil cooking spray

1. Heat oven to 350°. Spray three rehrücken pans (11¾-by-4½-inch loaf pans can also be used) lightly with cooking spray. Scatter almonds in pans. In bowl of electric mixer, beat butter, almond paste, confectioners' sugar, salt, vanilla, and lemon zest on medium-low speed, about 1 minute. Add egg yolks, one at a time, beating on medium-low speed for 1 minute after each. Beat in liqueur.
2. In a medium bowl, sift together cornstarch and flour.
3. Beat egg whites on medium-high speed until foamy, about 2 minutes. Gradually add granulated sugar, and beat on high speed until stiff peaks form, about 6 minutes.
4. Using a rubber spatula, fold half of the flour mixture into the egg-yolk mixture. Fold in half the egg whites. Fold in remaining flour mixture, then remaining egg whites, then chocolate and ginger.
5. Divide batter evenly among three pans.

Bake for 25 minutes, rotate pans between oven shelves, and bake about 25 minutes more; a cake tester inserted into the center of each loaf should come out clean. Let pans cool on a wire rack for about 5 minutes. Transfer loaves from pans to rack; let cool 20 minutes. Serve warm or at room temperature.

hartshorn COOKIES

makes about 50 cookies

Hartshorn powder, also known as baker's ammonia, is used instead of baking powder in these old-fashioned cookies; it gives them better flavor and texture.

- 1   *cup (2 sticks) unsalted butter, at room temperature*
- 1¼ *cups sugar*
- ½   *teaspoon pure almond extract*
- 1½ *cups all-purpose flour, sifted*
- 1   *teaspoon hartshorn powder or baking powder*
- ¼   *teaspoon salt*

1. Heat oven to 325°. In bowl of an electric mixer, cream butter and sugar on medium speed, about 4 minutes. Add the almond extract; beat until combined. Add flour, hartshorn or baking powder, and salt; beat on low speed to combine, about 1 minute, scraping down sides of bowl once.
2. Line two baking sheets with parchment. Roll a heaping teaspoon of dough into a ball, and place on baking sheet; repeat, placing balls 1 inch apart on baking sheets. Bake for 8 minutes, rotate pans between oven shelves, and bake for 8 to 10 minutes more; cookies should not brown. Transfer parchment with cookies to a wire rack to cool. Keep cookies in an airtight container if not serving right away.

almond TORTE

serves 8 to 10

10 tablespoons unsalted butter, melted, at
    room temperature, plus more for pans

1½ cups unblanched whole almonds

1 cup plus 2 tablespoons granulated sugar

¼ cup cornstarch

¼ cup all-purpose flour

1 teaspoon baking powder

¼ teaspoon salt

6 large eggs

¼ cup orange-flavored liqueur, such as
    Grand Marnier or Cointreau

1 cup best-quality seedless raspberry jam

⅓ cup confectioners' sugar, for sprinkling
    Vegetable-oil cooking spray
    Marzipan holly leaf and berries for
    decoration (optional)

1. Heat oven to 375°. Butter two 8-inch-round cake pans; line with parchment paper; butter parchment. In a food processor, process the almonds and granulated sugar to a powder. Sift together cornstarch, flour, baking powder, and salt.

2. In bowl of electric mixer, beat 2 eggs with almond-sugar mixture on low speed until blended, about 1 minute. Add remaining eggs, one at a time, beating on high speed for 3 to 4 minutes and scraping down sides of bowl after each egg. Beat in liqueur.

3. Sprinkle cornstarch mixture over egg mixture; fold in. Fold in melted butter. Pour batter into prepared pans. Bake 15 minutes, rotate pans between oven shelves, and bake 15 to 17 minutes more, or until cake tester inserted into the center of a cake comes out clean. Line two wire racks with parchment; spray paper with cooking spray. Turn cakes out of pans and onto parchment-lined racks; cool for 45 minutes.

4. In a small saucepan, warm jam over low heat, stirring occasionally. Spread warm jam on one cake layer; top with second layer, and dust with confectioners' sugar. Decorate with marzipan if desired.

ABOVE: This sugar-dusted almond torte, a homey yet elegant cake filled with raspberry jam, is decorated with holly leaves and berries shaped out of marzipan; it sits on an antique tole cake stand.

PERFECT ROASTING

THE BEST PRIME RIB & YORKSHIRE PUDDING

The keys to success with prime rib are knowledge, technique, and your trusty instant-read thermometer.

When buying prime rib, ask the butcher for the first cut—the first three ribs in the short end of the beef—and to trim and tie it. Ask for the short ribs, too; cooked with the roast, they add juice and flavor to the drippings.

While the roast is cooking, oven heat draws meat juices to the surface. For optimum flavor and slicing ease, the roast needs to rest once it's out of the oven, allowing the juices to redistribute through the roast.

Meanwhile, the same flavor-laden roasting pan used for the prime rib is ready for the Yorkshire pudding. The batter must be very cold and the roasting pan very hot: The reaction between the two makes the pudding puff.

For ingredients, cooking times, and more information, refer to the recipes on page 18.

1. PREPARING AND ROASTING THE PRIME RIB
Trim roast of excess fat. The butcher will cover top of roast with an extra, thin layer of fat, which should be left on; it bastes the roast as it cooks. Tie short ribs for easy handling. Let roast stand at room temperature for about 2 hours. Place short ribs and roast, fat-side up, in a heavy stainless-steel or other metal pan (preferably not nonstick). The rib bones are a natural rack; you won't need a metal one. Rub the meat all over with coarse salt and freshly cracked black pepper. Cook the roast on the lowest rack in a 450° oven for 20 minutes. Then reduce the oven to 325°, but don't open the door. For beef that's rare in the center and brown and crispy on the ends, cook for 1 hour and 25 minutes more. Check the internal temperature using an instant-read thermometer: Stick the probe halfway into thick end of the

ABOVE: A carved prime rib of beef, also called a standing rib roast, is surrounded by roasted shallots, pearl onions, and haricots verts. The word *prime* refers to the highest quality in the U.S. Department of Agriculture's grading of beef. Real prime beef is sold only in the best butcher shops and restaurants. Most grocers sell choice beef, which follows prime in the grading system. Have the butcher trim and tie your roast; it will cook better and make a grand presentation.

roast between two ribs, making sure that it's not near a bone. It will read 115° if the roast is done. If not, return the roast to the oven, and check temperature at 10-minute intervals, until it reaches 115°. (While roast is resting and the remainder of the meal is completed, the temperature will go up about 10° to reach 125°.)

2. POURING OFF DRIPPINGS Transfer the roast to a platter. Place near stove to keep warm; do not cover. Keep the short ribs as a snack or to use when making soup. Pour drippings from the pan into a fat separator.

3. DEGLAZING THE PAN Return roasting pan to medium-high heat. Carefully pour 1½ cups of good-quality dry red wine into the pan; bring to a boil, and use a wooden spoon to scrape off the crispy brown bits stuck to the pan. Turn down heat to medium, and cook until the liquid is reduced by half. Adjust seasoning to taste. Strain the juices through a fine sieve into a heatproof bowl. Cover the bowl; keep warm by placing the bowl in a barely simmering saucepan containing one inch of water.

4. POURING PUDDING BATTER INTO ROASTING PAN Add ¼ cup of reserved pan drippings from fat separator to roasting pan; heat pan in oven at 425° for 5 minutes. Quickly pour cold Yorkshire pudding batter into the hot pan. Bake until pudding has risen and is golden brown.

5. REMOVING RIBS AND CARVING ROAST While the pudding bakes, cut twine away from the roast. Arrange roast with bones perpendicular to platter. Grip the bones with one hand. With the other hand, slide a sharp knife straight down between the meat and the bones, separating the two as you cut down. Continue until the bones are completely separated. Transfer the roast to a serving platter where it can easily be sliced. A sharp carving knife is invaluable, making thick or thin slices only a matter of preference.

6. REMOVING YORKSHIRE PUDDING FROM OVEN Make sure the pudding is well browned before removing it from the oven. Undercooked pudding will taste raw and collapse quickly. Serve each person a large wedge of pudding with the crispy edge, which will hold its shape nicely.

THE BEST ROAST TURKEY & CLASSIC STUFFING

The plump and regal turkey is the quintessential American roast. Fortunately, achieving perfection isn't hard, especially if you follow these steps.

The best flavor comes from a fresh, unfrozen bird, preferably one raised without medicated feed and with a certain amount of strolling space in its pen. If your regular market can't help, ask your butcher or look in farmers' markets or health-food stores.

Before buying the turkey, check the size of your oven and roasting pan. You'll need a roasting pan small enough to fit your oven, large enough to fit the turkey, and two to three inches high. Since this pan will be used for many years to come, invest in a sturdy stainless-steel one that has a good heft to it—comfortably robust but not so heavy that with a twenty-pound turkey in it you can't move it. Avoid the disposable aluminum pans that hang like holiday tinsel in supermarket aisles this time of year. They're flimsy and dangerous, since it's far too easy to spill grease and burn yourself—or drop the turkey.

roast TURKEY

serves 12 to 25

A turkey this size generously serves twelve for dinner, or it can serve twice as many guests as part of a buffet.

1   twenty-to-twenty-one-pound fresh whole turkey, giblets and neck removed from cavity
1½   cups unsalted butter (3 sticks), melted, plus 4 tablespoons unsalted butter at room temperature
1   bottle dry white wine
2   teaspoons salt
2   teaspoons freshly ground pepper

1. GETTING STARTED A large turkey, like the 20-to-21-pound bird called for in this recipe, will cook much better, and have juicier flesh, than a smaller one. So even if you're serving fewer than twelve people for dinner, this large bird may still be the best choice, especially because you won't have to skimp on extra helpings—or on

ABOVE: This golden-brown turkey, just out of the oven and surrounded by roasted root vegetables and onions, is ready to be presented to holiday guests. Roast turkey makes a sumptuous main course for a full sit-down dinner with traditional side dishes like mashed potatoes and other favorite winter vegetables. For an open-house buffet, offer turkey with crusty rolls, mustards and chutneys, cheeses, and festive prepared salads.

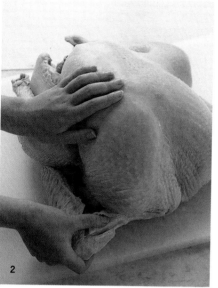

leftovers. The essential supplies include cheesecloth, kitchen string, a pastry brush, and an instant-read meat thermometer to tell you when meat is finished cooking. The cheesecloth will be soaked in melted butter and wine, then draped over the turkey as it cooks, ensuring a moist roast. Peppercorns and coarse salt season the bird.

2. PREPARING THE TURKEY Remove the giblets from the cavity. Rinse the bird in cool water, and dry with paper towels. Place rack on lowest level in oven; heat oven to 450°. Combine melted butter and white wine in a bowl. Fold a large piece of cheesecloth into quarters and cut it into a 17-inch, four-layer square. Immerse cheesecloth in the butter and wine; let soak. If the turkey comes with a pop-up timer, remove it; an instant-read thermometer is much more accurate. Fold wing tips under turkey. Sprinkle ½ teaspoon salt and ½ teaspoon pepper inside turkey.

3. STUFFING THE BIRD Prepare stuffing (see recipe on page 128). Insert the stuffing just before the turkey goes into the oven. Never do it ahead of time, and don't pack it too tightly; the stuffing won't cook evenly, and bacteria may grow. Fill the large cavity and the neck cavity loosely with as much stuffing as they can hold comfortably. Cook any remaining stuffing in a buttered baking dish for 45 minutes at 375°.

4. SECURING THE NECK FLAP Fold neck flap under, and secure with toothpicks.

5. TRUSSING Place turkey, breast-side up, on a roasting rack in a heavy metal roasting pan (preferably not nonstick); the rack will keep the turkey from sticking to the pan. Pull the legs together loosely, and tie them with kitchen string—a bow will be easy to untie later. Any kind of sturdy white string or twine will do, as long as it's made of cotton, not polyester, which may melt in the oven's heat. Rub turkey with the softened butter, and sprinkle with remaining 1½ teaspoons salt and 1½ teaspoons pepper.

6. COVERING WITH CHEESECLOTH Lift cheesecloth out of liquid, and squeeze it slightly, leaving it very damp. Spread it evenly over the breast and about halfway down the sides of

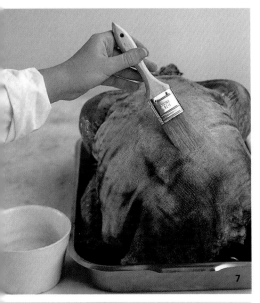

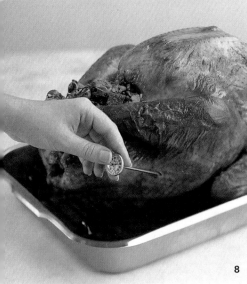

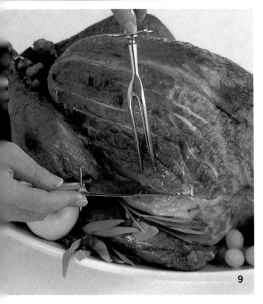

the turkey; it can cover some of the leg area. Place turkey, legs first, in oven. (If your roasting pan only fits sideways in the oven, turn the pan every hour so the turkey cooks and browns evenly.) Cook for 30 minutes.

7. BASTING After 30 minutes, use a pastry brush—which is more effective than a bulb baster—to baste the cheesecloth and any exposed parts of turkey with butter and wine. (The turkey pictured here is out of the oven, but basting should always be done in the oven and as quickly as possible so the oven temperature doesn't drop.) Reduce the oven temperature to 350°, and continue to cook the turkey for 2½ hours more, basting every 30 minutes, and watching pan juices; spoon some out if they are in danger of over-flowing. (Watch the cheesecloth carefully to make sure it does not dry out and burn; baste more often if necessary. If using an electric oven, make sure cheesecloth does not come into contact with heating element.) After the third hour of cooking, carefully remove and discard cheesecloth; it will have turned quite brown. Turn roasting pan so that the breast is facing the back of the oven. Baste turkey with pan juices. If there are not enough juices, continue to use the butter and wine. The skin gets fragile as it browns, so baste carefully. Cook 1 hour more, basting after 30 minutes.

8. TAKING THE TEMPERATURE After this fourth hour of cooking, insert an instant-read thermometer into the thickest part of the thigh. If the thermometer pokes a bone, try again. The temperature should reach 180° (stuffing should be at least 165°), and the turkey should be golden brown. The breast does not need to be checked for tem-perature. If the legs are not yet fully cooked, baste turkey, return to oven, and cook 20 to 30 minutes more. Total cooking time can vary due to moisture content of bird and to individual ovens. Convection ovens may cook more quickly.

9. CARVING When the turkey is fully cooked, transfer it carefully to a serving platter, and let it rest for about 30 minutes before carving. Use a thin-bladed, carbon-steel knife to carve the meat into thin slices.

classic STUFFING

makes 12 cups

The terms *stuffing* and *dressing* are often used interchangeably, but they do have different meanings: Stuffing is cooked inside the bird, dressing on its own.

- ¾ cup (1½ sticks) unsalted butter
- 4 onions (2 pounds), peeled and cut into ¼-inch dice
- 16 celery stalks, cut into ¼-inch dice
- 10 large fresh sage leaves, chopped, or 2 teaspoons crushed dried sage
- 6 cups homemade or low-sodium canned chicken stock
- 2 loaves stale white bread (about 36 slices), crust on, cut into 1-inch cubes
- 2 teaspoons salt
- 4 teaspoons freshly ground pepper
- 3 cups coarsely chopped flat-leaf parsley leaves (about 2 bunches)
- 2 cups pecans, toasted and chopped (optional)
- 2 cups dried cherries (optional)

1. Melt butter in a large skillet. Add onions and celery, and cook over medium heat until onions are translucent, about 10 minutes. Add sage, stir to combine, and cook 3 to 4 minutes. Add ½ cup stock, and stir well. Cook for about 5 minutes, until liquid has reduced by half.

2. Transfer onion mixture to a large mixing bowl. Add remaining ingredients, including the remaining stock; mix to combine.

THE BEST GLAZED HAM

There's nothing quite like a ham. With its rosy meat under a sweet-and-spicy glaze cooked crisp, it is one of the great holiday roasts.

Ham can mean the hind leg of a pig (a fresh leg of pork is sometimes called fresh ham), or any cut of pork that has been preserved. But usually it is a pig's hind leg that has been preserved with salt by dry-curing or brining, producing the characteristic dense texture, salty flavor, and distinctive color.

The roast shown here is a brine-cured and smoked ham with shank and leg bones left in. Whole hams like these weigh from twelve to twenty pounds and serve some fifty people as part of a buffet. If you're not expecting quite that many, choose the meaty butt half or bonier shank half, at six to ten pounds each.

Ninety-five percent of the hams sold in this country are cooked during processing and need to be heated to only 140° to develop the flavor and caramelize the glaze. If a ham isn't precooked, it will be labeled "Cook before eating" and should be baked until a meat thermometer registers 160° (thirty minutes per pound at 350°).

Some cooks remove the rind that covers the ham, and trim and score the fat before putting the meat in the oven. But leaving the rind on for most of the cooking time allows the layer of fat underneath to baste and flavor the meat. The rind can be cut off for the last hour of cooking, the fat trimmed and glazed.

Whether it's a brushed-on liquid or a patted-on mixture of crumbs and sugar, the glaze is almost always sweet, echoing the trace of sugar in the cure and setting off the salt and smoke of the meat. Because sugar burns so easily, add it during the final hour of cooking.

Cleaning up can be the hardest job of all if the cook neglects to line the pan with heavy-duty foil. More than one first-time ham cook has thrown away a blackened pan.

But it's worth it. If some of ham's allure comes from a crisp covering of caramelized fat, it's good to know that the meat under the fat has only 140 calories in a three-ounce serving: another reason to celebrate.

ABOVE: A whole smoked ham comes fully cooked, but is cooked again, allowing the glaze of sugar and spice to turn golden brown and crusty. Cooks often swear by their own glazes, but this one could convert even the most resolute; it is a beguiling mixture of cider, molasses, mustard, cardamom, fennel, brown sugar, cinnamon, ginger, and corn syrup. As part of a buffet, this roast, which is surrounded by kumquats, will serve as many as fifty guests, who can make use of biscuits (rear) to assemble little ham sandwiches.

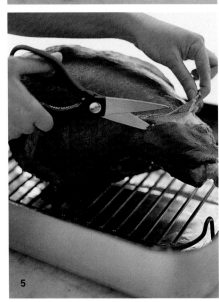

glazed HAM

serves 16 to 50

A ham this size can serve sixteen people for dinner and up to fifty for hors d'oeuvres.

1   *fourteen-to-eighteen-pound whole smoked ham, bone in and rind on*
1   *cup apple cider*
¼   *cup yellow mustard seeds*
2   *tablespoons whole cardamom pods*
1   *tablespoon whole fennel seeds*
2   *teaspoons ground cinnamon*
1   *tablespoon ground ginger*
¾   *cup prepared mustard*
1   *cup plus 2 tablespoons light-brown sugar*
¾   *cup dark-brown sugar*
3   *tablespoons light corn syrup*
2   *tablespoons unsulfured molasses*
2 to 3   *tablespoons whole cloves*
4   *fresh bay leaves (optional)*

1. GETTING STARTED Assemble ingredients for glaze. Rinse ham with cool water; dry with paper towels. Let stand for 2 hours at room temperature. Place rack on lowest level in oven; heat oven to 350°.

2. ROASTING THE HAM Line a roasting pan with heavy-duty aluminum foil. Place a roasting rack in pan. Transfer ham, with the thicker rind on top, to rack. Pour ½ cup cider over ham. Cook 2 hours, or until an instant-read thermometer registers 140°.

3. TOASTING AND GRINDING SPICES Meanwhile, toast mustard seeds, cardamom, and fennel in a heavy skillet over medium-low heat for 3 to 4 minutes, until aromatic. Transfer to spice mill or mortar and pestle; grind well.

4. FINISHING THE GLAZE Combine ground-spice mixture with cinnamon, ginger, mustard, 2 tablespoons light-brown sugar, 2 tablespoons dark-brown sugar, corn syrup, and molasses. Mix well; set aside.

5. REMOVING THE RIND Let ham cool for about 30 minutes. Using kitchen shears or a sharp knife, trim away the hard rind from the ham.

6. TRIMMING THE FAT With a sharp knife, carefully trim the fat to a layer of about

¼ inch all over the ham. The bottom side of the ham will have less fat and more skin. Place ham bottom-side down in the pan.

7. SCORING THE FAT Score the remaining fat on top of the ham into a pattern of 1- to 2-inch diamonds, making cuts about ¼ to ½ inch deep, through the fat and into the meat.

8. APPLYING THE GLAZE Insert a whole clove into the intersection of each diamond. Using a pastry brush or your fingers, rub the glaze all over the ham and into the cut diamonds.

9. COATING WITH SUGAR Combine remaining cup light-brown sugar and ½ cup plus 2 tablespoons dark-brown sugar. Use your hands to gently pack the sugar mixture all over scored fat. If you are using bay leaves, secure them with toothpick halves around the shank bone. Cover the toothpicks by inserting cloves on top of them.

10. BASTING THE HAM Return ham to oven, and cook for 20 minutes. Sugar will begin to crystallize, but there will be some hard spots of sugar; gently baste these areas with the remaining ½ cup cider; never baste with the pan juices as they will cloud the glaze. Cook 40 minutes more, basting with the remaining glaze after 20 minutes. The ham should be dark brown and crusty; cook 15 minutes more if necessary. Remove from oven, and let cool slightly. Transfer ham to a serving platter or carving board, and let stand about 30 minutes before carving.

11. STARTING TO CARVE Cookware shops sell specialized ham knives with long, thin blades, but any sharp knife with a long blade will do. An electric knife with twin serrated blades does the job remarkably well. Before carving, cut a few thin slices from the side of the ham that is rounder and protrudes more. Stand the ham on this cut side; the meatiest part of the ham is now on top, ready to be sliced. (It will still be slightly unsteady, however, so make sure to carve carefully.) Now, slice straight down in ¼-inch intervals until you hit the bone.

12. REMOVING THE SLICES In one motion, run the knife horizontally along the top of the bone. Slices will lift out easily and can be placed, overlapping, on a serving platter.

TEMPLATES

ROYAL-ICING SNOWFLAKES Use these to make the ornaments shown on page 54. Photocopy the templates, enlarging or reducing them if you wish. For the best results, don't make the snowflakes larger than five inches across, or they will become too fragile.

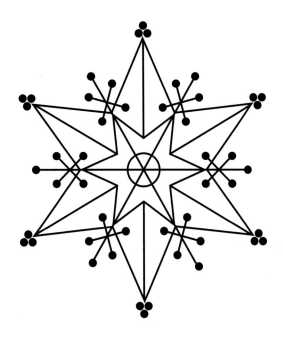

STOCKING AND FELT PROJECTS The oak leaf and daisy templates are the actual sizes used for the bottle bag (page 104) and daisy stocking (page 106)—though of course you can enlarge or reduce them if you wish. The scallop edge can be used to finish felt pillows, bags, boxes, and other creations.

For the stockings (pages 106 to 109) enlarge a template to desired size on a photocopier. For a stocking with a cuff, make sure the cuff and stocking are enlarged in the same proportions. Before cutting out the felt, refer to the detailed instructions for the stocking you want to make—some require adding a seam allowance when cutting the fabric. To attach a cuff, sew ends of the two cuff pieces together, forming a loop. Slip the cuff inside the stocking so the smaller side of the loop is flush with the top, sew together around the top, and turn down the cuff on the outside. To finish the stocking, add a loop for hanging.

PLACE ON FOLD

OAK LEAF

DAISY

BOOT STOCKING

SCALLOP EDGE

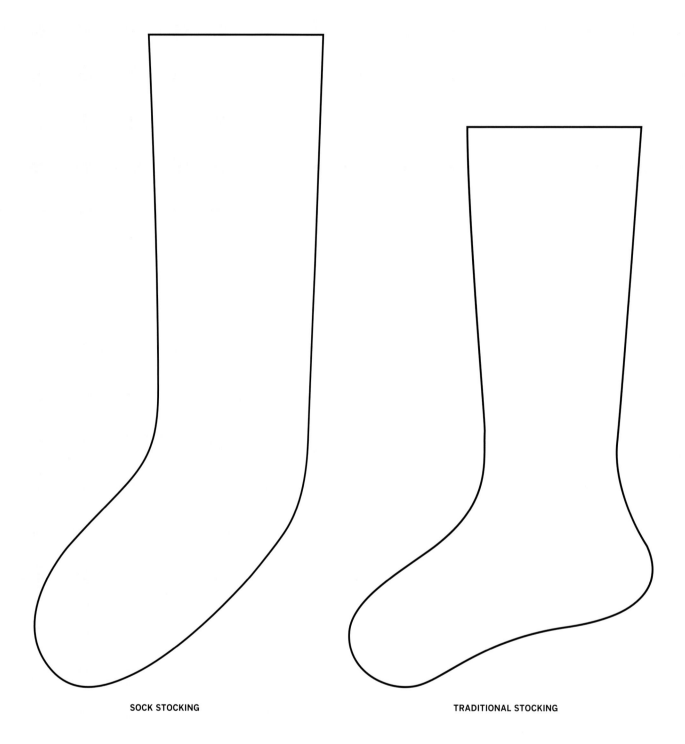

SOCK STOCKING

TRADITIONAL STOCKING

THE GUIDE

Items pictured but not listed are from private collections. Addresses and telephone numbers of sources may change prior to or following publication, as may price and availability of any item.

COVER

French Art Deco nickeled-bronze lyre-shaped **candelabra**, *from Marvin Alexander, Inc., 315 East 62nd Street, New York, NY 10021; 212-838-2320. To the trade only.* Custom **silver leafing**, *by Franco Eliali, 909 40th Street, #2, Brooklyn, NY 11219; 718-871-1167.*

MARTHA'S CHRISTMAS FEAST

Pages 12 to 22
Custom **silver leafing**, *by Franco Eliali, see above.*

Page 12
Antique Venetian **mirror**, *from Consignmart, 877 Post Road East, Westport, CT 06880; 203-226-0841.* Louis XV-style

marble-top table, c. 1900, $5,600, *from Rooms & Gardens, 290 Lafayette Street, New York, NY 10012; 212-431-1297.* American handblown crystal **decanter**, $200, *from David Stypmann Co., 192 Sixth Avenue, New York, NY 10013; 212-226-5717.* Glass **candleholders** by Mathias, $125 to $425, *from Takashimaya, 693 Fifth Avenue, New York, NY 10022; 212-350-0100 or 800-753-2038.* **Acacia baileyana and pink-pepperberry garlands**, $16 per foot, *from Green Valley Growers, 10450 Cherry Ridge Road, Sebastopol, CA 95472; 707-823-5583.* Chair **upholstery**, *by Tony Totilo, 219 Belltown Road, Stamford, CT 06905; 203-323-4490.* **Linen rug**, $4,000, *from Harmil Carpet, Inc., 969 Third Avenue, New York, NY 10022; 212-838-1330. To the trade only.*

Page 13
Victorian clear-glass **smoke bell**, $395, *from AERO, 132 Spring Street, New York, NY 10012; 212-966-1500.*

Page 14
French Art Deco nickeled-bronze lyre-shaped **candelabra**, *from Marvin Alexander, Inc., 315 East 62nd Street,*

New York, NY 10021; 212-838-2320. To the trade only.

Page 15
Irish-crystal **water carafe** with stars, $200, and hand-cut crystal **decanter**, $125, *from David Stypmann Co., see above.*

Page 16
Crystal **champagne glasses**, *from Consignmart, see above.*

Page 17
Quinces, *available seasonally from:* Dean & DeLuca, 560 Broadway, New York, NY 10012; 212-226-6800. Sid Wainer & Son Specialty Produce & Specialty Foods, 2301 Purchase Street, New Bedford, MA 02746; 508-999-6408 or 800-423-8333. *Free catalog.*

Page 20
American 1850s blown-glass **trifle bowl**, *from Nancy Boyd, 2466 Main Street, P.O. Box 866, Bridgehampton, NY 11932; 516-537-3838.*

Page 22
Oval **bobeche centerpiece with candleholders**, *from The Dining Trade, 306 East*

61st Street, New York, NY 10021; 212-755-2304. Blown-glass **vase/candleholder** by Mathias, *from Takashimaya, see above.*

Page 23

Handblown glass **candelabra** by Mathias, $380, *from Intérieurs, 114 Wooster Street, New York, NY 10012; 212-343-0800.*

FLOWERS & GREENERY

Page 28

15"-to-18" **dwarf spruce** and **fir trees,** *from Rosedale Nurseries, Saw Mill River Road, Hawthorne, NY 10532-1598; 914-769-1300.* **National Christmas Tree Association,** *611 East Wells Street, Milwaukee, WI 53202; 414-276-6410. Free brochure. http://www.christree.org*

Pages 30 to 33

Florist Michael George New York, *315 East 57th Street, New York, NY 10022; 212-751-0689.*

Pages 34 to 36

Poinsettias, *from Paul Ecke Ranch, P.O. Box 230488, Encinitas, CA 92023.*

Page 37

Pinecones, $4.95 for 5-to-6-ounce sack, *from Galveston Flower Wreath Co., 1124 Twenty-fifth Street, Galveston, TX 77550; 409-765-8597 or 800-874-8597.*

GARLANDS & ORNAMENTS

Page 41

36-gauge **aluminum foil,** $6.50 per 10' sheet; 20-gauge **wire,** $2.80 per spool; and **metal snips,** $12.60 to $22.75; *all from Metalliferous, 34 West 46th Street,*

New York, NY 10036; 212-944-0909. **Metal Projects Kit,** $28, *from Martha By Mail; 800-950-7130.* Silver **foil paper,** 85¢ per sheet, *from New York Central Art Supply, 62 Third Avenue, New York, NY 10003; 212-473-7705 or 800-950-6111.*

Page 42

36-gauge **aluminum foil,** $6.50 per 10' sheet, and Jax aluminum **blackener,** $20, *from Metalliferous, see above.* Custom monogrammed **embossers,** *from:* Empire Stamp & Seal, *36 East 29th Street, New York, NY 10016; 212-679-5370 or 800-988-7826.* Martha By Mail; *800-950-7130.* **Crinkle wire,** $3 per yard, *from D. Blümchen, P.O. Box 1210, Ridgewood, NJ, 07451-1210; 201-652-5595.*

Page 44

Silver **foil paper,** 85¢ per sheet, and colored **craft papers,** *from New York Central Art Supply, see above.* **Two-sided papers,** *from Kate's Paperie, 561 Broadway, New York, NY 10012; 212-633-0570.*

Page 45

16" **topiaries,** $35 each, *from Fischer & Page, 136 West 28th Street, New York, NY 10001; 212-645-4106.* Mirror-topped **coffee table,** $3,900; striped **chair,** $4,500; and **sofa,** $5,200; *all from Mariette Himes Gomez Associates, 506 East 74th Street, New York, NY 10021; 212-288-6856.* **Fire tools,** $225, *from Brian Windsor Art, Antiques, and Garden Furnishings, 272 Lafayette Street, New York, NY 10012; 212-274-0411.* 1840s English bamboo **side table** with antique papier-mâché tray, $4,775, *from Nancy Corzine, 305 East 63rd Street, New York, NY 10021; 212-758-4240.*

Pages 46 and 47

Metallic and **patterned papers,** 50¢ to $5, *from New York Central Art Supply, see above.* Fiskars **pinking shears,** $6,

from Sax Arts & Crafts, P.O. Box 51710, New Berlin, WI 53151; 800-558-6696. Catalog, $5. **Wired tinsel,** $10 for 10', *from D. Blümchen, see above.* Vintage **silver trim,** $3 to $10 per yard; **tassel,** $3.50; and **silver ball,** $2; *all from Tinsel Trading, 47 West 38th Street, New York, NY 10018; 212-730-1030.*

Page 48

Mirror-backed sconces, $2,700 per pair, *from John Rosselli International, 523 East 73rd Street, New York, NY 10021; 212-772-2137. To the trade only.* Louis XVI mahogany **dining table,** $22,500, *from Reymer-Jourdan Antiques, 29 East 10th Street, New York, NY 10003; 212-674-4470.* English **stone urns,** $4,500 per pair, *from Treillage, Ltd., 418 East 75th Street, New York, NY 10021; 212-535-2288.* "Serlig" **aluminum chandelier,** $49, *from IKEA; 410-931-8940 for East Coast locations, 818-912-1119 for West Coast.*

Page 49

Paper-covered wire, $2.65 per 12' roll, *from Loose Ends, P.O. Box 20310, Salem, OR 97307; 503-390-7457 or 800-390-9979.* Colored **craft papers,** *from New York Central Art Supply, see above.*

Page 50

Reproduction **springerle molds,** $14 to $65, *from House-on-the-Hill, P.O. Box 7003, Villa Park, IL 60181; 708-969-2624. Brochure, $2.* Vintage **number molds,** $8.50 each, *from Urban Archaeology, 285 Lafayette Street, New York, NY 10012; 212-431-6969.* **Paper clay,** $12 per pound, *from Sax Arts & Crafts, see above.* **Paper Clay Kit,** *from Martha By Mail; 800-950-7130.*

Pages 50 and 51

Special thanks to Malinda Johnston of Lake City Crafts and to Rosemary Muench.

Quilling tool, $2.50, and ⅛" **quilling paper**, $2.45 for 50 strips, *from Lake City Crafts, P.O. Box 2009, Nixa, MO 65714; 417-725-8444.* **Silver thread**, 80¢ to $2.65 per yard, *from Kate's Paperie, see above.* **Recommended reading:** Malinda Johnston, *The Book of Paper Quilling: Techniques and Projects for Paper Filigree* (Sterling, 1994; $21.95).

Page 52

Cast-iron urn, $1,200 per pair, *from Treillage, Ltd., see above.* Calvert reproduction **demilune table**, $4,050, *from Nancy Corzine, see above.*

Page 53

¼" **quilling paper**, $2.45 for 50 strips, *from Lake City Crafts, see above.* Colored **craft papers**, *from New York Central Art Supply, see above.* **Two-sided papers**, *from Kate's Paperie, see above.*

Page 54

Meringue powder, $5.99 for 10 ounces, and decorative **silver dragées**, $5 for 4 ounces, *from New York Cake & Baking Distributor, 56 West 22nd Street, New York, New York 10010; 212-675-2253 or 800-942-2539.*

Page 55

Assorted **cookie cutters**, $3 to $12, *from New York Cake & Baking Distributor, see above.* **Snow Crystal copper cookie cutter**, $45 (includes Prancing Reindeer cookie cutter), and **Star copper cookie cutter**, $45 (includes Man in the Moon cookie cutter), *from Martha By Mail; 800-950-7130.*

Page 56

German **glass peach**, $175, *from Kelter Malcé Antiques, 74 Jane Street, New York, NY 10014; 212-675-7380.*

Page 57

German **blown-glass storks** on clip, $75

to $85; **bird** on clip, $20; large German **glass Santa**, $75; **blown-glass ball**, $40; American **shiny brights**, $3 to $5; and large **glass balls** with cardboard caps, $3 to $5; *all from Main Street Antiques, 156 Main Street, Flemington, NJ 08822; 908-788-6767.* Small German **glass Santa**, $45; red **grapes**, $600; golden **pear**, $250; and ribbed green **Kugel**, $750; *all from Kelter Malcé Antiques, see above.* German **Kugels** and green **blown-glass oblong**, $120; all *from J. Goldsmith Antiques, 1924 Polk Street, San Francisco, CA 94109; 415-771-4055.* **Glass bell**, $8; **glass tree** with crushed-glass frost, $10; **glass ball** with pink stripe, $8; and **glass lantern** with crushed-glass frost, $8; *all from Linda Rosen Antiques at the Tomato Factory Annex, Hopewell, NJ 08525; 609-466-9833.*

Page 58

Czechoslovakian **glass-bead boat**, $48, *from Main Street Antiques, see above.* Japanese **cardboard-and-glitter house**, $12.50, *from Linda Rosen Antiques, see above.* Czechoslovakian **glass-bead diamond**, $9 to $12, *from J. Goldsmith Antiques, see above.*

Page 59

German **blown-glass flower basket**, $85 to $90; red **blown-glass-and-crimped-wire bauble**, $45; Japanese tiny **glass acorn**, $7 to $10; tiny **glass pinecone**, $7 to $10; and German **glass snowman**, $37; *all from Main Street Antiques, see above.* **Gilt-paper-and-lithograph angel**, $175; **crepe-paper-and-cardboard angel**, $95; **camel**, $45; and German **paper-and-glass acorns**, $55; *all from Kelter Malcé Antiques, see above.* Gold-and copper-**tinsel snowflake**, $24; **carpet bag**, $285; **sheep**, $110; American **blown-glass walnut** with glitter, $3.50; and Japanese **cotton-and-plastic snowman**, $28; *all from J. Goldsmith Antiques, see above.* **Stork**, $250; **ladies'**

slipper, $165; and **gun**, $275; *all from Barbara Trujillo Antiques, 2466 Main Street, P.O. Box 866, Bridgehampton, NY 11932; 516-537-3838.* German **glass-bead, cotton, and paper snowman**, about $30, *from U.S.E.D., 17 Perry Street, New York, NY 10014; 212-627-0730.*

MERINGUE

Pages 62 to 73

Assorted Ateco **pastry tips**; *800-645-7170 for nearest retailer.*

COOKIES & CANDIES

Page 77

Reproduction **springerle molds**, $14 to $65, *from House-on-the-Hill, P.O. Box 7003, Villa Park, IL 60181; 630-969-2624. Brochure,* $2. French **rolling pin**, $13; fluted **pastry cutters**, $3.75 for 2" round; and **cookie sheets**, $18; *all from Bridge Kitchenware, 214 East 52nd Street, New York, NY 10022; 212-688-4220 or 800-274-3435.*

Page 78

30"-by-40" **sheet plastic**, $24, *from Canal Plastics, 345 Canal Street, New York, NY 10013; 212-925-1032.* ¼" antique **metallic ribbon**, $2 per yard, *from Tinsel Trading, 47 West 38th Street, New York, NY 10018; 212-730-1030.*

Page 79

Wood veneer, $7.75 per sheet, *from New York Central Art Supply, 62 Third Avenue, New York, NY 10003; 212-473-7705 or 800-950-6111.* Linen **book-binding cord**, $9 per spool, *from Talas, 568 Broadway, New York, NY 10012; 212-219-0770. Catalog,* $5.

Page 82

Rose water, $7 for 4 ounces; **citric acid,** $4 for 4 ounces; **orange-flower water,** $16 for 33 ounces; **lemon, apricot,** and **anise oils,** $2 for 2 drams; *all from New York Cake & Baking Distributor, 56 West 22nd Street, New York, NY 10010; 212-675-2253 or 800-942-2539.*

Page 83

Cedar **brush box,** $29, *from Pearl Paint, 308 Canal Street, New York, NY 10013; 212-431-7932 or 800-221-6845.* **Organdy ribbon,** $1 to $6 per yard, *from Kate's Paperie, 561 Broadway, New York, NY 10012; 212-633-0570.* Small **glassine envelopes,** $1.60 for 25, *from Apec, 900 Broadway, New York, NY 10003; 212-475-1204 or 800-221-9403.*

Page 85

Transparent papers, $1 per sheet, *from New York Central Art Supply, see above.* **Half-sheet pan,** $13, *from Bridge Kitchenware, see above.*

Page 87

Small **chocolate cup molds** (G190), $8.75 per tray, *from Tomric Plastics, 136 Broadway, Buffalo, NY 14203; 716-854-6050.*

Page 88

Assorted chocolate molds, *from Rosie's Cake and Candy Closet, 40 McDermott Avenue, Riverhead, NY 11901; 516-727-8965.* 3" **foil squares,** $3 for 125 sheets, *from New York Cake & Baking Distributor, see above.* **Jewel-shape chocolate molds** (#J25), $2.50 per tray, *from Candyland Crafts, 201 West Main Street, Somerville, NJ 08876; 908-685-0410.*

Page 89

Domino and **card-suit chocolate molds,** $2 per tray, *from:* The Gingham House, *310 Grand Avenue, Billings, MT 59101;*

406-252-6138. Sweet Celebrations, *7009 Washington Avenue South, P.O. Box 39426, Edina, MN 55439; 612-943-1661 or 800-328-6722 .*

Pages 90 and 91

Valrhona chocolate, $20 per 2-pound bar; **Callebaut chocolate,** $8 per pound; **ice chipper,** $9; 8" **offset spatula,** $2.50; **square scraper,** $5; 8" **pastry bag,** $1.50; *all from from New York Cake & Baking Distributor, see above.* **Ghirardelli chocolate,** $8 per pound, *from the Ghirardelli Chocolate Company; 800-877-9338 for nearest retailer.* **Carma chocolate coins,** $11.24 for 23 ounces, *from Enclosures: Chocolate; 800-225-6651. Free catalog.* Antique ceramic **chemist's bowl,** $125, *from Wolfman-Gold & Good Company, 117 Mercer Street, New York, NY 10012; 212-431-1888.* **Dome-shape chocolate mold,** *from Rosie's Cake and Candy Closet, see above.*

Pages 92 and 93

6" **alphabet chocolate molds,** $2 per tray, *from:* The Gingham House, *see above.* Sweet Celebrations, *see above.* **Parchment paper,** $4 per 20' roll, *from New York Cake & Baking Distributor, see above.* **Egg** (#13) and **acorn and oak-leaf chocolate molds** (#Ao68), $2.50 per tray, *from Candyland Crafts, see above.* 14" **bronze platter,** $250, *from William Lipton, 27 East 61st Street, New York, NY 10021; 212-751-8131.* Mother-of-pearl **caviar spoon,** $12, *from Dean & DeLuca, 560 Broadway, New York, NY 10012; 212-431-1691 or 800-221-7714. Free catalog.*

GIFTS & WRAPPING

Pages 96 to 111

Scissors and shears, *from:* Mundial,

Inc.; 800-487-2224 for nearest retailer. Fiskars; *800-950-0203 for nearest retailer.* **Pinking shears,** $33 to $37, *from Steinlauf & Stoller, 239 West 39th Street, New York, NY 10018; 212-869-0321.*

Page 96

Glassine, $11.25 for a 48"-by-10" roll, *from Utrecht Art and Draft Supplies, 33 35th Street, Brooklyn, NY 11232; 800-223-9132.* **Ribbons,** *from Hyman Hendler & Sons, 67 West 38th Street, New York, NY 10018; 212-840-8393.*

Page 97

Balsam, $6 for 1 pound, $50 for 10 pounds, $250 for 50 pounds, *from:* Asplin Tree Farm, *R.F.D. 1, Box 169A, Saranac Lake, NY 12983; 800-858-7336.* Martha By Mail; *800-950-7130.* Waxed **kozo paper,** $2.30 for 21"-by-31" sheet, or unwaxed, $1.02, *from New York Central Art Supply, 62 Third Avenue, New York, NY 10003; 212-473-7705 or 800-950-6111.*

Page 98

Tulle, $1.95 per yard, *from B&J Fabrics, 263 West 40th Street, New York, New York 10018; 212-354-8150.* **Ribbon,** *from C.M. Offray & Son, Inc., Route 24, Chester, New Jersey 07930; 908-879-4700.* **Wired tinsel,** $10 for 10', *from D. Blümchen & Company, P.O. Box 1210M, Ridgewood, NJ 07451; 201-652-5595.*

Page 100

Embossing powders, $3.50 to $3.90, *from Personal Stamp Exchange; 707-588-8058 for nearest retailer.* **Embossing supplies,** *from Hampton Art Stamps, 19 Industrial Boulevard, Medford, NY 11763; 516-924-1335 or 800-229-1019.*

Page 101

Christmas-tree cookie cutter, $3, and **alphabet set,** $35, *from Bridge Kitchen-*

ware, *214 East 52nd Street, New York, NY 10022; 212-688-4220 or 800-274-3435.*

Pages 102 to 107
Special thanks to the American Sales Corporation, distributor of Pfaff Creative sewing machines; 201-262-7211 for nearest dealer.
1mm **wool felt** in moss, melon, red, gray, pine green, light blue, and ecru, $18 per square yard; 2mm **wool felt** in ecru, $9 per half yard; and **Stocking Kit,** $68; *all from Martha By Mail; 800-950-7130.* **Synthetic felt,** $4.05 per yard, *from Central Shippee, Inc., 46 Star Lake Road, Bloomingdale, NJ 07403; 800-631-8968.* **Buttons,** 25¢ to $1.69 each, *from Hersh Buttons, 1000 Sixth Avenue, New York, NY 10018; 212-391-6615.* Three-ply **Persian wool yarn,** 55¢ per 5½-yard skein ("Floralia" in ecru), *from Herrschners, 2800 Hoover Road, Steven's Point, WI 54492; 715-341-8686 or 800-441-0838.*

Page 103
4" **organdy ribbon,** *from Midori; 800-659-3049 for nearest distributor.*

Pages 104 and 105
Large **eyelet kit,** $2.25, *from Greenberg & Hammer, 24 West 57th Street, New York, NY 10019; 212-246-2467.* **Silk piping,** $3 to $4 per yard, *from M&J Trimmings, 1008 Sixth Avenue, New York, NY 10018; 212-391-9072.*

Page 107
4¼" **polka-dot ribbon,** $14 per yard, *from Bell'occhio, 8 Brady Street, San Francisco, CA 94103; 415-864-4048.* 2⅝" **velvet ribbon,** $10 per yard, *from Hyman Hendler & Sons, see above.*

Page 108
Linen and cotton **dish towels,** $8 to $20, and 71"-by-110" linen **tablecloth,** $190,

from Ad Hoc Softwares, 410 West Broadway, New York, NY 10010; 212-925-2652.

Pages 110 and 111
Live plants, fruits, and produce may be subject to shipping restrictions between certain states. Check with your local post office for details.
³⁄₁₆" Astrogreen recycled **Bubble Wrap,** $46.80 for 175' roll, *from Consolidated Plastics Co., 8181 Darrow Road, Twinsburg, OH 44087; 216-425-3900 or 800-362-1000.* **Wood excelsior,** $10 to $12 per 5-pound box, *from Western Excelsior Corp., 901 Grand Avenue, P.O. Box 659, Mancos, CO 81328; 970-533-7412.* Biodegradable **foam peanuts,** $11 per bag, *from Clean Green Packing Company of Minnesota, 720 Florida Avenue, Golden Valley, MN 55426; 612-545-5400.* **Eco-Foam,** $3 per bag, *from American Excelsior; 800-326-3626 for nearest distributor.* **Prancing Reindeer copper cookie cutter,** $45 (includes Snow Crystal cookie cutter), *from Martha By Mail; 800-950-7130.* **Packing information hotlines:** DHL, *800-225-5345;* Federal Express, *800-463-3339;* United Postal Service, *800-742-5877;* United States Postal Service, *888-275-8777.*

NEW YEAR'S DAY AT HOME

Page 113
Stacked 8", 10", and 12" **cake stands,** $99 for set of three, *from Martha By Mail; 800-950-7130.*

Pages 114 to 123
Green peppercorn pâté, $10 per pound, *from Les Trois Petits Cochons, 453 Greenwich Street, New York, NY 10013; 800-537-7283.* **Monukka raisins,** $2.65 per pound; **glacéed citron melons,**

$4.50 per pound; **glacéed kiwi,** $9.50 per pound; **cinnamon almonds,** $5.50 per pound; **toffee mixed nuts,** $3.55 per pound; *all from A. L. Bazzini, 339 Greenwich Street, New York, NY 10013; 212-334-1280 or 800-228-0172. Free catalog.* **Smoked hams,** $4.39 per pound, *from Kurowycky Meat Products, 124 First Avenue, New York, NY 10009; 212-477-0344.* **Specialty-food catalogs:** Harry and David, *P.O. Box 712, Medford, OR 97501; 800-547-3033.* Neiman Marcus, *P.O. Box 650589, Dallas, TX 75265-0589; 800-825-8000.* Basse's Choice Plantation, Ltd., *P.O. Box 1, Smithfield, VA 23431; 800-292-2773.* Shelburne Farms, *102 Harbor Road, Shelburne, VT 05482; 802-985-8686.* Balducci's, *424 Sixth Avenue, New York, NY 10011; 800-572-7041.* Petrossian, *3342 Melrose Avenue, Roanoke, VA 24017; 800-828-9241.* Zingerman's, *422 Detroit Street, Ann Arbor, MI 48104-1118; 313-663-3354.*

Page 114
Visiting cards, $60 for 12, *from Mrs. John L. Strong Fine Stationery, 699 Madison Avenue, New York, NY 10021; 212-838-3775.*

Page 120
Purple **hurricane lampshade,** $2,200 for two, *from L. Becker Flowers, 217 East 83rd Street, New York, NY 10028; 212-439-6001.* Stacked 8", 10", and 12" **cake stands,** $99 for set of three, *from Martha By Mail; 800-950-7130.*

Page 122
12"-by-4" **rehrücken pans,** $9.50, *from Lamalle Kitchenware, 36 West 25th Street, New York, NY 10010; 212-242-0750.* **Hartshorn powder** (baker's ammonia), $4 for 8 ounces, *from Sweet Celebrations,*

7009 *Washington Avenue South, P.O. Box 39426, Edina, MN 55439; 612-943-1661 or 800-328-6722.*

PERFECT ROASTING

Pages 124 and 125
Roti **roasting pan,** *from All-Clad; 800-255-2523 for store locations.* **Instant-read thermometer,** $11.90, and 4-cup **fat separator,** $14.95, *from*

Bridge Kitchenware, 214 East 52nd Street, New York, NY 10022; 212-838-6746 or 800-274-3435.

Pages 126 to 128
Plastic **cutting board,** $34.95, *from Lamalle Kitchenware, 36 West 25th Street, New York, NY 10010; 212-242-0750. Catalog, $3.* **Roasting pan,** $41.20; Wüsthof 8" **curved-tine fork,** $66.75; and 10" **carving knife,** $63; *all from Bridge Kitchenware, see above.*

Page 129
10" **cake stand,** $37, *from Martha By Mail; 800-950-7130.*

Pages 130 and 131
Roasting pan, $41.20, *from Bridge Kitchenware, see above.* Plastic **cutting board,** $34.95; Wüsthof 8" **curved fork,** $73.95; and **ham slicer,** $67.50; *all from Lamalle Kitchenware, see above.*

PICTURE CREDITS

PHOTOGRAPHY

William Abranowicz
page 9

Melanie Acevedo
page 29 (left)

Anthony Amos
front cover, back cover (bottom row, right), pages 12, 13, 14, 15, 16, 17, 18, 19, 20, 21, 22, 23, 24, 25, 30, 31, 32, 33, 142 (center)

Christopher Baker
pages 127, 128

Antoine Bootz
back cover (top row, center), pages 27 (top left and right), 37, 54, 55, 94, 95, 97 (top), 98 (top), 109, 135 (center)

Anita Calero
pages 77, 79 (bottom), 82, 83 (right)

Carlton Davis
pages 74, 75, 76, 78, 79 (top row), 83 (left), 84, 85, 102, 103, 104, 105, 106 (bottom), 107

Reed Davis
pages 124, 125, 129, 130, 131

Gentl & Hyers
pages 2, 3, 10 (top), 11 (bottom), 38, 39, 40, 41 (top left and right), 42, 43, 46, 47, 50, 96, 97 (bottom), 99, 106 (top), 112, 113, 114, 115, 116, 117, 118, 119, 120, 121, 122, 123, 135 (left and right)

Thibault Jeanson
pages 5, 8, 26, 27 (middle and bottom), 44 (top), 45, 48, 49, 52

Stephen Lewis
back cover (top row, left), pages 6, 28, 101, 108

James Merrell
pages 80, 81 (bottom), 98 (bottom), 100

Victoria Pearson
back cover (top row, right), pages 60, 61, 62, 63, 64, 65, 66, 67, 68, 69, 70, 71

Randy Plimpton
page 4

Maria Robledo
pages 81 (top), 126

Victor Schrager
back cover (bottom row, center), pages 7, 11 (top and middle), 41 (bottom left), 44 (left), 51, 53 (top row), 56, 57, 58, 59, 86, 87, 88, 89, 90, 91, 92, 93, 142 (left)

Matthew Septimus
pages 72, 73

Evan Sklar
back cover (bottom row, left), pages 10 (bottom), 34, 35, 36, 142 (right)

Jonelle Weaver
pages 110, 111

Elizabeth Zeschin
page 29 (second, third, and fourth from left)

ILLUSTRATIONS

Harry Bates
pages 41, 44, 50, 53

INDEX

*If you have enjoyed this book,
please join us as a subscriber to
MARTHA STEWART LIVING magazine.
Call toll-free 800-999-6518.
The annual subscription rate
is $26 for 10 issues.*